CHOCOLATE

First published in Great Britain by Simon & Schuster UK Ltd, 2003
A Viacom Company

Simon & Schuster UK Ltd
Africa House
64–78 Kingsway
London
WC2B 6AH

1 3 5 7 9 10 8 6 4 2

Design: **Fiona Andreanelli**
Typesetting: **Stylize Digital Artwork**
Food photography: **Steve Baxter**
Home economist: **Joss Herd**
Stylist for food photography: **Liz Belton**
Editor: **Deborah Savage**
Printed and bound in China

ISBN 0 74324 012 X

Best-kept Secrets of the Women's Institute

CHOCOLATE

Sîan Cook

SIMON & SCHUSTER
A VIACOM COMPANY

ACKNOWLEDGEMENTS

There are so many people I would like to thank. First and foremost, I would like to thank my family – they are my life and without their support I would not have been able to produce the book. My husband, Terry, has helped me enormously with everything IT. He and Holly have put up with my jubilation when recipes have turned out as planned and my despair when they haven't. As always the constructive comments of my friends and family have been invaluable in creating successful recipes.

I would also like to thank Green and Black's and The Chocolate Society for supplying me with quantities of their wonderful chocolate (Valrhona from the Chocolate Society) for creating the recipes. Both were incredibly generous in sending me such excellent chocolate – it was as if Christmas had arrived early!

CONTENTS

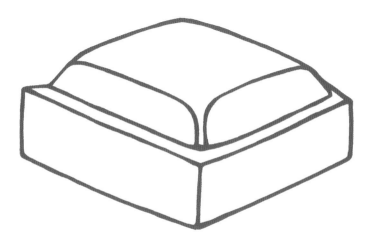

INTRODUCTION

How **lucky** I have been these last few weeks. I have been able to **indulge my obsession** with chocolate without any feelings of guilt! I did wonder, when I began the book, if my **passion** for chocolate would diminish while having to cook with it most days. I am pleased to say that this is not the case.

My love affair with chocolate is unscathed. In fact my passion for chocolate hasn't abated over many years, although it did falter during both pregnancies. I need to have chocolate at regular intervals, so I make sure a steady supply is ready to hand: chocolate is kept in my car and in my handbag, as well as secret places in the house which my daughter, Holly, tries to search out!

What is it about chocolate that makes it so seductive? For me, it has to be its velvety, rich, sweet flavour. Chocolate is the one luxury that we can all afford. It appeals to all ages and is a gift guaranteed to be gratefully received! John G. Tullius, American artist and cartoonist, once said, "Nine out of ten people like chocolate. The tenth person always lies".

Chocolate originated in Central America, in particular, Mexico, where it was regarded as an aphrodisiac by the Aztecs. There, it was consumed heavily spiced and unsweetened as a drink. When chocolate arrived in Europe in the 17th century, it was used to make a sweet drink and soon became popular in specialist places, similar to the coffee houses. In the early 19th century, a man called Van Houten came up with the first solid chocolate bar. From this time, chocolate began to be bought as confectionery and used in baking. In the 1840s, a Quaker company called Fry became the first manufacturers of chocolate confectionery in this country.

The status of chocolate in recent years has reached new heights and, in 1991, The Chocolate Society was formed. It is dedicated to promoting chocolate as one of the world's gourmet delights and to encouraging us to eat chocolate that is both better and healthier than the cheaper varieties. One of the brands of chocolate it endorses is Valrhona – which is described as a 'grand cru', a description normally associated with champagne and other fine wines.

A recent survey of European chocolate consumption revealed that the average Briton consumed 11.2 kg (24.7 lbs) of chocolate last year. To put it into context,

this is the equivalent of 266 Mars Bars! The UK chocolate consumption accounts for nearly a third of the European market. French and Swiss chocolate has a higher cocoa solid content than most British chocolate and therefore tends to be an acquired taste for many of us. In British chocolate a proportion of cocoa butter and milk is replaced with vegetable fat, which is why it has a greasy texture in the mouth.

I am sure that you will be pleased to learn that chocolate is good for you! It can protect you from heart disease as it contains anti-oxidants which lower low-density lipoproteins – 'bad' cholesterol in other words. In a recent study in America, two groups of volunteers were fed a typical diet, but one group was also given plain chocolate and cocoa. The group consuming chocolate and cocoa were found to have a greater anti-oxidant level than the first group, so their cholesterol was less prone to oxidation that leads to the hardening of the arteries, and their 'good' cholesterol was higher.

TYPES OF CHOCOLATE

Plain/Dark contains 30%–75% cocoa solids and is normally used in cooking. The higher the cocoa solids, the richer the flavour.

Milk chocolate has a milder, creamy flavour and tends to be sweeter than plain chocolate. It is made with dried milk powder and is more sensitive to heat than dark chocolate, so care needs to be taken when melting it.

White chocolate is technically not chocolate as it contains no cocoa solids – it is made from cocoa butter, milk and sugar and, as with milk chocolate, it is sensitive to heat. Therefore, always buy a luxury white chocolate when cooking with it.

Couverture chocolate has a high proportion of cocoa butter that gives a glossy appearance to confections. It is very expensive. It is mainly used by professionals.

Cocoa Powder is created when the cocoa powder has been pressed from the roasted and ground beans. As its flavour is unsweetened and bitter, it gives a good chocolate flavour when used in cooking.

Chocolate Chips are available in plain, milk and white and are designed to retain their shape when used in baking. They are therefore ideal for use in such recipes as muffins and cookies.

ADDING FLAVOURS

Chocolate combines so well with many other flavours. In the past, such flavours as chilli, vanilla and cinnamon were added, but nowadays there are so many to choose from: orange, raspberries, cherries and coffee to name but a few. Chocolate is also enhanced by alcohol such as brandy, whisky, rum, Amaretto and coffee-based liqueurs such as Tia Maria. White chocolate is a relative newcomer to the scene and cardamom combines wonderfully with it.

MELTING CHOCOLATE

The most important thing to remember is that chocolate doesn't like to be overheated. Overheated chocolate won't set properly or blend well. Another rule is that chocolate should not be melted over direct heat, except when it is with other ingredients, and even then it should be placed over a very low heat.

When you are melting chocolate, you should never be in a rush. I know that this is often difficult when we all lead such busy lives. However, the best results will always be when chocolate has been allowed to melt very slowly – it will then have a glossy appearance and the flavour will be perfect.

The best way of melting chocolate is to use a double-boiler. Break the chocolate into pieces and place them in a bowl that fits tightly over a pan of hot water. The bowl should not touch the water and no steam or drops of water should come into contact with the chocolate. Once the chocolate begins to melt, stir it. Once it has nearly melted, remove it from the pan and stir gently just once or twice until it has melted completely (the bowl will retain some heat and this will help complete the melting process).

It is also possible to melt chocolate in the microwave. Place the chocolate pieces in a microwaveable bowl. The time taken to melt the chocolate will depend on the type and quality of chocolate as well as the power of your microwave. As a general guide, 115 g (4 oz) plain chocolate will take 2 minutes on full power and milk and white chocolate will take 2–3 minutes on medium power. Stir the chocolate and leave it to stand for a few minutes. If it hasn't melted completely, you will need to return it to the microwave for about 30 seconds.

CHOCOLATE DECORATIONS

Grating chocolate is an easy and quick way to decorate your cake or dessert. Alternatively, drag a potato peeler along the edge of a bar of chocolate to create little curly shavings. However chocolate scrolls lend such a professional touch. Melt 100 g bar of chocolate in a bowl over a pan of barely simmering water. When it is melted pour the chocolate on to a marble slab or back of a baking sheet. Leave for about half an hour until it is just set. Now place the blade of a long, sharp knife at the edge of the chocolate and push away from you at a 45° angle so that the chocolate curls into scrolls.

I hope that you will enjoy preparing and eating the recipes in this book as much as I did creating and tasting them. To ensure that you get the best possible results, I would urge you always to use the best chocolate that you can buy, such as organic plain chocolate that contains at least 70% cocoa solids and luxury white chocolate. It's well worth the extra expense and you will notice the difference.

Few people can resist a chocolate cake or gâteau. They are certain to be popular at any special occasion – some couples even opt for one instead of the more traditional fruit cake at their wedding. Children of all ages tend to choose a chocolate cake for their birthday. In this chapter there are some familiar recipes that have been given a

CAKES & GÂTEAUX

makeover, such as Chocolate Battenburg Cake and a couple of speedy ones like Quick Chocolate Cake and Refrigerator Cake. There are also more elaborate and time-consuming recipes (but I hope you will agree, well worth the effort) such as Death by Chocolate and Chocolate Mousse Gâteau.

SERVES 8
PREPARATION & COOKING TIME:
30 minutes and 20–25 minutes cooking

This gâteau should appeal to all chocolate lovers.

If in season, a selection of fresh berries would make a delicious contrast to the rich chocolate.

BLACK & WHITE CHOCOLATE GÂTEAU

3 large eggs
80 g (3 oz) caster sugar
60 g (2¼ oz) plain flour
½ teaspoon baking powder
15 g (½ oz) cocoa powder,
plus extra for dusting
150 g (5 oz) white chocolate,
broken into squares
25 g (1 oz) unsalted butter
300 ml (10 fl oz) double cream, whipped
55 g (2 oz) amaretti biscuits, crushed
30 ml (2 tablespooons) Amaretto (optional)

1   Preheat the oven to Gas Mark 4/180°C/350°F. Grease and line 2 x 20 cm (8-inch) sandwich cake tins.

2   Put the eggs and sugar in a large bowl and whisk until the mixture becomes thick and pale – the whisk should leave a thick trail when lifted. Sift the flour, baking powder and cocoa together.

3   Using a metal spoon, fold the flour mixture into the egg mixture quickly and evenly. Divide between the cake tins and spread it out lightly. Bake for 20–25 minutes, until the cake springs back when pressed gently with the fingertips. Turn it out and cool on a wire rack.

4   While the cake is baking, put the white chocolate in a large bowl placed over a pan of gently simmering water. When the chocolate has melted, stir in the butter and continue to stir until it has melted. Allow the mixture to cool and then fold in the cream. Reserve half of this white chocolate cream and fold the amaretti biscuits into the other half.

5   To assemble, place one sponge cake on a serving plate and sprinkle it with the Amaretto, if using, and then spread over the amaretti chocolate cream. Place the second sponge on top and cover this with the white chocolate cream, making a swirling pattern with a fork. Dust with a little sieved cocoa powder.

SERVES 8–10
PREPARATION & COOKING TIME:
50 minutes + 25–30 minutes cooking
FREEZING: recommended

What can I say about this gâteau? It is totally decadent and over the top and, therefore, **a dream cake for all chocoholics!** It involves using a number of bowls (and finger-licking) but it's well worth the effort involved. Serve with lashings of cream and mugs of real hot chocolate – if you're going to be indulgent, you might as well do it in style.

FOR THE CAKE:
175 g (6 oz) margarine
275 g (10 oz) light muscovado sugar
3 eggs, beaten lightly
5 ml (1 teaspoon) vanilla extract
250 g (9 oz) plain flour, sifted
1 tablespoon baking powder
150 ml (5 fl oz) soured cream
50 g (2 oz) white chocolate, melted
20 g (¾ oz) cocoa powder, sifted
50 g (2 oz) plain chocolate, melted

FOR THE ICING AND FILLING:
200 g (7 oz) plain chocolate, broken into pieces
100 g (3½ oz) unsalted butter, diced
100 ml (3½ fl oz) double cream
4 tablespoons good quality plain chocolate spread
80 g (3oz) white chocolate, cut into small pieces
100 g bar of white chocolate, to decorate

1 Preheat the oven to Gas Mark 5/electric oven 190°C/fan oven 170°C. Grease and line the base of three 20 cm (8-inch) sandwich tins.

2 Whisk the margarine and sugar together until thick and creamy. Add the eggs a little at a time, whisking well between each addition. Add the vanilla extract, flour, baking powder and soured cream, and mix together thoroughly.

3 Transfer a third of the creamed mixture to another bowl and fold in the melted white chocolate, a little at first and then the remainder. Spoon this into one of the sandwich tins, levelling the surface. Add the cocoa powder and melted plain chocolate to the remaining mixture and, again, mix thoroughly. Divide this mixture between the other two sandwich tins and level the surfaces.

4 Bake in the oven for 25–30 minutes, until the sponges have risen and they are firm to the touch. Leave to cool in the tins for 5 minutes and then transfer to a wire rack to cool completely.

5 While they are cooling, make the icing. Melt the plain chocolate in a bowl set over a pan of barely simmering hot water. Remove it from the heat, add the diced butter and stir until the butter has melted. Add the cream gradually, stirring continuously – the mixture will immediately start to thicken. Allow it to cool so that it is of a spreadable consistency.

6 Place one of the two dark chocolate sponges on to a plate and spread the surface with half of the chocolate spread. Scatter half the white chocolate pieces over the spread. Place the white chocolate sponge on top, right way up and spread the top with the remaining chocolate spread. Scatter the remaining white chocolate pieces over the spread and place the third sponge on top. Spoon the icing on the top, and, using a palette knife, spread it evenly all over the top and sides of the gâteau. Make scrolls with the white chocolate bar (see page 9), or grate it if you prefer, and scatter over the top.

DEATH BY CHOCOLATE

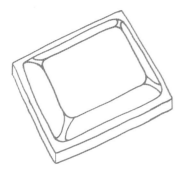

SERVES 8–10
PREPARATION & COOKING TIME:
40 minutes + 30 minutes cooking
FREEZING: recommended

My daughter, Holly, loves Battenburg cake and, as a chocoholic, I thought she would adore this cake – and she did! It is important to use a good quality spread so that the chocolate flavour can really be tasted. The cheaper chocolate-flavour brands also tend to have too thin a consistency.

115 g (4 oz) soft margarine
115 g (4 oz) caster sugar
2 eggs, beaten lightly
100 g (3½ oz) ground almonds
115 g (4 oz) self-raising flour
5 ml (1 teaspoon) vanilla extract
2 tablespoons cocoa powder, sifted
45 ml (3 tablespoons) milk
100 g jar of dark chocolate spread
cornflour, for dusting
225 g (8 oz) marzipan, white or golden

CHOCOLATE BATTENBURG CAKE

1 Preheat the oven to Gas Mark 4/electric oven 180°C/fan oven 160°C. Grease and line the base and short sides of two 450 g (1 lb) loaf tins.

2 Place the margarine, sugar, eggs, ground almonds, flour and vanilla extract in a bowl and beat with an electric whisk until the ingredients are all combined and the mixture is smooth. Place half the mixture in another bowl. Add the cocoa powder to one bowl with 30 ml (2 tablespoons) of milk. Add the remaining milk to the other bowl and beat both mixtures well.

3 Spoon the cocoa mixture into one loaf tin and the plain mixture into the other, making a slight dip in the middle so that the cakes rise evenly. Bake in the oven for 30 minutes until they are firm to the touch and the blade of a knife inserted into the cakes comes away clean. Remove the cakes from the tins after a few minutes and allow to cool on a rack.

4 Cut each cake in half lengthways and trim them so that they are even. Sandwich the four pieces together with chocolate spread to create a chequerboard effect.

5 Dust a work surface with some cornflour. Roll out the marzipan to a rectangle large enough to wrap around the cake. Smooth some chocolate spread evenly over the marzipan. Wrap the marzipan around the cake, making sure the seam is underneath, and press the edges together to seal them. Cut the cake into slices with a sharp knife – this is easier to do when the cake has been wrapped in foil and chilled for a little while – to reveal the pattern.

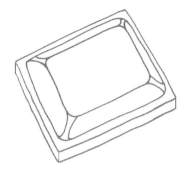

SERVES 8–10
PREPARATION & COOKING TIME:
40 minutes + 1 hour chilling
+ 30 minutes cooking
FREEZING: recommended

This is a cross between a cake and a dessert and would be suitable both for serving with tea or as the finale of a dinner party. The sponge is very light, and the addition of melted butter makes it moist.

FOR THE SPONGE:
4 eggs
115 g (4 oz) caster sugar
100 g (3½ oz) plain flour, sifted
15 g (½ oz) cocoa powder, sifted
40 g (1½ oz) butter, melted

FOR THE MOUSSE:
150 g (5 oz) plain chocolate,
    broken into pieces
15 ml (1 tablespoon) medium
    or sweet sherry
1 teaspoon gelatine powder
3 eggs, separated
300 ml (10 fl oz) whipping cream,
    whipped to soft peaks
50 g (1¾ oz) caster sugar
2 tablespoons chocolate spread
cocoa powder or grated chocolate,
    to decorate

CHOCOLATE MOUSSE GÂTEAU

1 Preheat the oven to Gas Mark 4/electric oven 180°C/fan oven 160°C. Grease a 20 cm (8-inch) cheesecake tin or loose-bottomed cake tin and line the base with baking parchment.

2 Make the sponge by placing the eggs and sugar in a large bowl set over a pan of hot water. Whisk them for about 10 minutes, until the mixture is thick and creamy. Remove the bowl from the heat and continue to whisk for 1 minute. Sprinkle the flour and cocoa over the surface and fold them in gently with a metal spoon using a figure-of-eight action. When they are nearly all incorporated, add the melted butter and mix it in.

3 Pour the mixture into the prepared tin. Bake for 25–30 minutes until the cake has risen, is firm to the touch and

beginning to come away from the sides. Allow to cool in the tin for 5 minutes. Remove the cake from the tin and then cool completely on a wire rack. Slice it in half horizontally.

4 To make the chocolate mousse, place the chocolate and sherry in a bowl set over a pan of hot water and allow to melt; stir and leave to cool.

5 Meanwhile, put 15 ml (1 tablespoon) of cold water in a medium bowl and sprinkle the gelatine over. Leave for a few minutes and then place the bowl in a larger bowl of hot water and stir to dissolve the gelatine. Alternatively, place the bowl in the microwave on full power for 15 seconds. Allow the mixture to cool and then beat in the egg yolks, one at a time, followed by the melted chocolate mixture and half the cream.

6 Whisk the egg whites until they are fairly stiff and then continue to whisk while adding the sugar, a teaspoon at a time. Add 1 tablespoon to the chocolate mixture to loosen it, then carefully fold in the remaining egg whites.

7 Smooth the chocolate spread over the cut surface of the top half of the gâteau and place it back in the cake tin, chocolate spread upwards. Spoon the chocolate mousse on top and place this in the fridge to set for about 1 hour.

8 Place the other sponge half on top, cut side on to the chocolate mousse. Spread the remaining cream on top and sprinkle with either cocoa powder or grated chocolate. Leave it in the cake tin until you are ready to serve.

SERVES 8–10
PREPARATION & COOKING TIME:
45 minutes + 30 minutes cooking
FREEZING: recommended

A really good Black Forest Gâteau is something special. It is a little time-consuming to make but well worth the effort – the appreciative '**oohs**' and '**ahs**' from my fellow Mencap directors when I served it at a board meeting were testimony to that! It freezes well, but I would recommend that you decorate it with the reserved cherries after it is defrosted.

FOR THE SPONGE:

4 eggs
115 g(4oz) caster sugar
95 g (3½ oz) plain flour, sifted
15 g (½ oz) cocoa powder, sifted
40 g (1½ oz) butter, melted

FOR THE FILLING AND DECORATION:

2 x 425 g tins of black cherries in syrup, drained, reserving 225 ml (8 fl oz) syrup
30 ml (2 tablespoons) kirsch
1 tablespoon arrowroot
250 g tub of Quark
300 ml (10 fl oz) double cream
2 tablespoons icing sugar
130 ml (¼ pint) cream, for piping rosettes
115 g (4 oz) chocolate, to make scrolls (see page 9)

1   Preheat the oven to Gas Mark 4/electric oven 180°C/fan oven 160°C. Grease a 20 cm (8-inch) cheesecake or loose-bottomed tin and line the base with baking parchment.
2   Make the sponge by whisking the eggs and sugar together in a large bowl set over a pan of hot water for about 10 minutes, until the mixture is thick and creamy. Remove the bowl from the heat and continue to whisk for 1 minute. Sift together the flour and cocoa over the surface of the mixture and fold it in gently, using a figure-of-eight action. When it is nearly all incorporated, add the melted butter and mix it in. Pour the mixture into the prepared tin. Bake for 25–30 minutes, until the cake starts coming away from the sides and is fairly firm to the touch.
3   Allow the cake to cool in the tin for 5 minutes and then turn it out on to a cooling rack and allow to cool completely. Cut it twice horizontally to create three equal layers. Place the top layer on a serving plate, cut side upwards.
4   Mix (30 ml) 2 tablespoons of the reserved cherry syrup with the kirsch and sprinkle this over the three layers. Mix a further 2 tablespoons of the reserved syrup with the arrowroot. In a small saucepan, bring the remaining syrup to boiling point, and then stir in the arrowroot mixture. Heat gently until the syrup thickens. Remove the pan from the heat. Reserve 12 cherries and cut the rest in half. Add the halved cherries to the thickened syrup and allow the mixture to get cold.
5   Place the Quark in a mixing bowl and beat it to loosen it slightly. Whip the cream to soft peaks. Fold a quarter of the cream into the Quark. Spread this evenly on the sponge on the plate and the middle sponge layer. Divide the cherry mixture between these two sponge layers, but don't spread it right to the edges. Place the middle sponge on top of the bottom layer and then top with the remaining sponge layer.
6   Spoon the remaining cream on top and spread it over the entire gâteau, making sure there is no sponge visible. Use the cream to pipe rosettes around the gâteau and decorate with the reserved cherries and chocolate scrolls.

BLACK FOREST GÂTEAU

SERVES 12–15
PREPARATION & COOKING TIME: 10 minutes +1½ hours cooking
FREEZING: recommended

MAKES 12 slices
PREPARATION TIME: 30 minutes + 3 hours chilling
FREEZING: recommended

CHOCOLATE CHRISTMAS CAKE

REFRIGERATOR CAKE

This moist cake would make a great alternative to the traditional fruit Christmas cake. The chocolate flavour doesn't dominate, but gives the cake a lovely rich flavour. It takes minutes to prepare – ideal for such a hectic time of year. I would suggest cutting it into small, thin slices as it is quite a rich cake.

400 g (14 oz) luxury mincemeat
225 g (8 oz) mixed dried fruit
200 g (7 oz) plain flour, sifted
25 g (1 oz) cocoa powder, sifted
3 level teaspoons baking powder
3 eggs
150 g (5½ oz) soft margarine
150 g (5½ oz) demerara sugar
15 ml (1 tablespoon) milk (if needed)
50 g (2 oz) milk chocolate, cut into small pieces
50 g (2 oz) pecan or walnuts, chopped
80 g (3 oz) whole blanched almonds

1 Preheat the oven to Gas Mark 3/electric oven 170°C/fan oven 150°C. Grease and line the base of a 900 g (2 lb) loaf tin.
2 Place all the ingredients, except the chocolate, pecan or walnuts, almonds and milk in a large mixing bowl and beat them together well, until everything is well blended. If the mixture seems a little dry, add 1 tablespoon of milk.
3 Stir the chocolate pieces and pecans or walnuts into the bowl and then spoon the mixture into the tin. Level the surface using the back of the spoon. Arrange the almonds in a circle around the edge of the cake.
4 Bake in the oven for about 1½ hours or until the centre of the cake is firm to the touch. Allow to cool in the tin for a few minutes and then transfer the cake to a wire rack to finish cooling.

This is such an easy recipe, ideal for children to make. You can adapt the recipe to suit your tastes or what you have available in your cupboard. Cut into small pieces, it is delicious served with coffee after dinner. Store the pieces in an airtight tin and they will keep for a couple of weeks, but they never last that long in our house!

115 g (4 oz) butter
2 tablespoons golden syrup
175 g (6 oz) plain chocolate pieces (Green and Black's Maya Gold gives a hint of orange)
225 g (8 oz) Rich Tea biscuits, broken into very small pieces, but not crumbs
50 g (2 oz) glacé cherries, quartered
25 g (1 oz) dried apricots, cut into small pieces
50 g (2 oz) blanched almonds, chopped finely
50 g (2 oz) white chocolate, broken into small pieces

1 Place the butter, syrup and chocolate in a large bowl, set it over a pan of barely simmering water and allow the mixture to melt, stirring from time to time. Remove the bowl from the heat and allow to cool a little.
2 Add the biscuits, cherries, apricots and almonds and mix thoroughly. Finally, fold in the white chocolate pieces.
3 Lightly oil a large loaf tin and line with clingfilm. Spoon the chocolate mixture into the tin and press down firmly. Place in the fridge for a few hours to set and harden. Turn out the cake on to a board and, using a sharp knife, cut into slices.

SERVES: 6–8
PREPARATION & COOKING TIME:
15 minutes + 30 minutes cooking
FREEZING: recommended

QUICK CHOCOLATE CAKE

Some chocolate cakes do not actually taste of chocolate, but this one has a **lovely deep flavour**. The fact that it takes minutes to prepare is an added bonus. I have suggested using apricot jam for the filling, but any other fruit jam would be fine, particularly raspberry or black cherry.

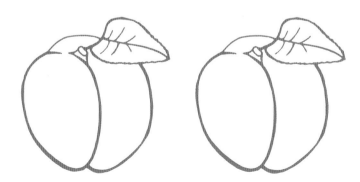

FOR THE CAKE:
175 g (6 oz) self-raising flour
65 g (2½ oz) cocoa powder
1 heaped teaspoon baking powder
115 g (4½ oz) light muscovado sugar
150 ml (5 fl oz) sunflower oil
150 ml (5 fl oz) milk
2 eggs

FOR THE FILLING:
30 ml (2 tablespoons) lemon juice
80 g (3 oz) light muscovado sugar
225 g (8 oz) cream cheese
apricot jam
icing sugar, sifted, for dusting

1　Preheat the oven to Gas Mark 3/electric oven 160°C/fan oven 140°C. Grease two 18 cm (7-inch) sandwich tins and line the bases with baking parchment.
2　Place all the ingredients for the cake in a large mixing bowl and mix well – if using an electric whisk, start on the lowest setting. Divide the mixture between the two tins, level the surfaces and bake in the oven for 25–30 minutes, until the sponges have risen and are firm to the touch. Leave to cool in the tins for a few minutes and then remove them from the tins to a cooling rack to cool completely.
3　Place the lemon juice, muscovado sugar and cream cheese in a bowl and mix thoroughly. Place one sponge half on a plate, cut side up and spread thickly with the jam. Spoon the cream cheese mixture on top and carefully spread it over the jam. Place the other sponge on top. Dust with icing sugar.

These make wonderful desserts for special occasions as they look so impressive. The recipes here such as Mississippi Mud Pie or White Chocolate and Raspberry Tart are great for a dinner party or a buffet especially as they can be prepared in advance. The pastry in the tarts and pies can be changed to suit your taste. If you

TARTS, PIES & CHEESECAKES

don't feel confident to make your own pastry or don't have enough time, simple cheat by buying ready-made pastry or pastry cases. For cheesecake lovers, there are three to choose from: Chocolate and Clementine Cheesecake, Tiramisù Cheesecake or Warm White and Dark Chocolate Cheesecake – all deliciously different.

This is a wonderful dessert to offer chocolate lovers at **Christmas time**. The clementines add a seasonal flavour and are natural partners for chocolate. It is very rich so serve in fairly small wedges.

CHOCOLATE & CLEMENTINE CHEESECAKE

225 g (8 oz) clementines, unpeeled
25 g (1 oz) caster sugar
175 g (6 oz) chocolate digestive biscuits, crushed
50 g (2 oz) butter, melted
675 g (1½ lb) curd cheese
3 large eggs
80 g (3 oz) soft brown sugar
225 g (8 oz) plain chocolate, broken into squares
150 ml (5 fl oz) single cream

TO DECORATE:
whipped cream
1 peeled clementine
cocoa powder

1 Wash the clementines and place them in a saucepan. Cover them with water and bring to the boil. Simmer for 25 minutes until the fruit is tender. Drain the clementines and purée them with the caster sugar. Set aside.

2 Preheat the oven to Gas Mark 2/electric oven 150°C/fan oven 130°C. Combine the biscuit crumbs and butter and spoon this into a greased 20 cm (8-inch) cheesecake tin. Press down (a potato masher does this well) and place the tin in the fridge to chill.

3 Beat the curd cheese, eggs and soft brown sugar together.

4 Melt the chocolate and cream together in a bowl over a pan of gently simmering water. Allow the chocolate mixture to cool and then fold it into the curd cheese mixture.

5 Spoon the cheesecake mixture over the biscuit base. Put dollops of the clementine purée on top of the cheesecake and swirl with a skewer or pointed knife.

6 Bake in the oven for 1¼–1½ hours until it is set. Allow the cheesecake to cool in the switched-off oven. Chill in the fridge for at least 2 hours. To decorate, spread whipped cream over the surface, arrange some clementine segments on top and dust with sifted cocoa powder.

  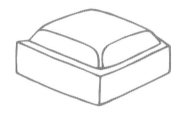

SERVES 6
PREPARATION & COOKING TIME:
30 minutes + 30 minutes chilling
+ 25 minutes cooking
FREEZING: recommended

Crisp buttery pastry, filled with a dark chocolate cream makes eating this tart **a heavenly experience!** It is delicious served by itself, or you could accompany it with some raspberries and cream.

CHOCOLATE GANACHE TART

FOR THE PASTRY:
175 g (6 oz) plain flour
80 g (3 oz) butter, diced
80 g (3 oz) caster sugar
3 egg yolks

FOR THE FILLING:
300 ml (½ pint) double cream
225 g (8 oz) plain chocolate,
broken into pieces
40 g (1½ oz) butter
1 tablespoon brandy (optional)
icing sugar, to decorate

1   To make the pastry, place the flour, butter and sugar in a food processor and pulse until the mixture resembles breadcrumbs. Add the egg yolks and process briefly until the mixture starts to come together. Wrap the dough in clingfilm and place it in the fridge for 30 minutes. If you don't have a food processor, rub the butter into the flour in a bowl, stir in the sugar and then add the yolks and mix until the dough is formed.

2   Preheat the oven to Gas Mark 4/electric oven 180°C/fan oven 160°C. Roll out the pastry on a floured work surface and use it to line a 20 cm (8-inch) loose-bottomed tart tin. Prick the base with a fork. Line the pastry with baking parchment or foil and fill with baking beans.

3   Bake the pastry case for 10 minutes. Remove the parchment or foil and

beans, and continue to bake for a further 10–15 minutes until the pastry is golden and cooked. Allow to cool in the tin on a wire rack.

4   To make the filling, place the cream in a medium saucepan and bring it to the boil over a moderate heat. Remove the pan from the heat and add the chocolate pieces. Stir until the chocolate is melted and then add the butter, stirring until the butter has melted. Add the brandy, if using, and mix it in. Pour the filling into the cooled pastry shell and smooth it so that the surface is level. Allow to cool and then chill in the fridge until ready to serve.

5   Remove from the fridge 30 minutes before serving, so that it is at room temperature. Dust the surface with sifted icing sugar.

The '**mud**' in the title of this well-known American dessert refers to the muddy waters of the Mississippi area, hence the dark chocolate, fudgy filling. There are many interpretations of this deliciously rich dessert – mine is similar to a baked cheesecake.

SERVES 8
PREPARATION & COOKING TIME:
25 minutes + 50 minutes cooking
FREEZING: recommended

MISSISSIPPI MUD PIE

FOR THE BASE:
115 g (4 oz) digestive biscuits, crushed to fine crumbs
50 g (2 oz) butter, melted
25 g (1 oz) granulated sugar

FOR THE FILLING:
200 g (7 oz) plain chocolate, broken into pieces
200 g (7 oz) butter, diced
200 g (7 oz) light muscovado sugar
4 eggs
300 ml (10 fl oz) single cream

FOR THE TOPPING:
225 ml (8 fl oz) double cream, whipped
cocoa powder, for dusting

1 Preheat the oven to Gas Mark 5/electric oven 180°C/fan oven 160°C.

2 Combine the crushed biscuits, melted butter and sugar and mix well. Spoon this into a greased 20 cm (8-inch) cheesecake or loose-bottomed cake tin and press it down.

3 To make the filling, place the chocolate and butter in a medium saucepan and melt over a very, very gentle heat, stirring from time to time. Remove the pan from the heat and stir in the sugar, followed by the eggs, one at a time. When they are incorporated, stir in the cream. Pour the mixture on to the biscuit base and bake in the oven for 50 minutes or until the filling is set and just firm. Allow to cool before removing from the tin (it will sink a little).

4 When the pie has cooled, spread the whipped cream over the top and dust lightly with sifted cocoa powder.

SERVES 6
PREPARATION TIME:
20 minutes + 2 hours chilling
FREEZING: not recommended

Bananas and toffee are natural partners in Banoffee Pie. Adding chocolate to this **winning combination** creates a fabulous dessert for those with a very sweet tooth. You can prepare the base a day in advance and the filling a couple of hours before serving, but the banana decoration needs to be done at the last minute.

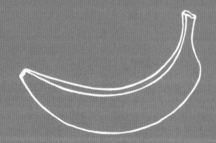

I tablespoon cocoa powder
100 g (3½ oz) butter, melted
250 g (9 oz) plain chocolate digestive biscuits, crushed to fine crumbs
4 oz (115 g) plain chocolate, cut into pieces
4 firm bananas
450 g jar of banoffee toffee sauce
425 ml (¾ pint) double cream, whipped
grated chocolate or cocoa powder, to decorate

1 Stir the cocoa powder into the melted butter and stir to dissolve. Mix in the biscuit crumbs and mix thoroughly. Spoon this into a 20 cm (8-inch) cheesecake tin or loose-bottomed cake tin and press down firmly – a potato masher helps do this. Chill for I hour.

2 Melt the chocolate in a bowl over a pan of barely simmering hot water. Allow to cool.

3 Slice two of the bananas and arrange them on the biscuit base. Fold the melted chocolate into the banoffee sauce and mix well. Fold a third of the cream into the sauce and spread it over the sliced bananas. Chill for I hour more.

4 Spread the remaining cream on top of the pie. Just before serving, slice the remaining two bananas and arrange them on top of the cream. Sprinkle either some grated chocolate or sifted cocoa over the cream.

CHOCOLATE BANOFFEE PIE

These tartlets look so attractive with their contrasting colours: the pale pastry is topped with a layer of dark chocolate with a filling of white chocolate. A raspberry coulis would be a delicious accompaniment to this elegant dessert.

SERVES 4
PREPARATION & COOKING TIME:
40 minutes + 50 minutes chilling
+ 25 minutes cooking
FREEZING: recommended

FOR THE PASTRY:
175 g (6 oz) plain flour
25 g (1 oz) cornflour
80 g (3 oz) butter, diced
50 g (2 oz) icing sugar
1 egg and 1 egg yolk

FOR THE MOUSSES:
115 g (4 oz) plain chocolate
175 g (6 oz) white chocolate,
broken into pieces
45 ml (3 tablespoons) milk
2 teaspoons gelatine
225 ml (8 fl oz) double cream,
whipped to soft peaks
2 egg whites
2 drops lemon juice
cocoa powder, for dusting

DOUBLE CHOCOLATE MOUSSE TARTLETS

1 Place the flour, cornflour, butter and icing sugar in a food processor and process until the mixture resembles breadcrumbs. Add the egg and egg yolk, together with 1 teaspoon of cold water and process until a dough forms. Wrap the dough in clingfilm and place in the fridge for 30 minutes.

2 Divide the dough into six pieces and roll each piece out on a floured surface to fit six 10 cm (4-inch) loose-bottomed flan tins. Prick the bases with a fork and trim the edges. Line the pastry cases with baking parchment or foil and fill with baking beans. Chill for a further 20 minutes.

3 Preheat the oven to Gas Mark 4/electric oven 180°C/fan oven 160°C. Bake for 10 minutes, remove the parchment or foil and beans and return to the oven for a

further 10–15 minutes, until the pastry is golden brown and cooked. Cool completely on a wire rack.

4 Melt the plain chocolate and brush the insides of the pastry cases with it – it's better to brush a thin layer and then repeat rather than brushing one thick layer. Leave to set.

5 Place the white chocolate and milk in a bowl and set the bowl over a pan of barely simmering hot water. Stir occasionally until the chocolate has melted. Allow to cool. In a small dish, sprinkle the gelatine over 1 tablespoon of cold water and leave for the mixture to go spongy. Dissolve the gelatine by setting the bowl in a larger bowl of hot water or place in the microwave for 10 seconds. Stir until no crystals are visible. Allow to cool.

6 Add the gelatine to the white chocolate mixture and mix well. Fold in the whipped cream. Whisk the egg whites with the lemon juice until they are stiff. Add a spoonful of the whisked egg whites to the chocolate mixture and mix it in. Fold in the remaining egg whites using a figure-of-eight action.

7 Spoon the mousse into a piping bag fitted with a star nozzle and pipe the mixture into the tart cases (alternatively simply spoon the mousse into the cases). Dust the tartlets with sifted cocoa powder.

Coffee combined with chocolate is a classic combination. The mocha filling is a mousse that makes this dessert lighter than you would expect. You will need a few mixing bowls – but you won't mind the extra washing up once you have tasted this.

SERVES 6
PREPARATION & COOKING TIME:
35 minutes + 50 minutes chilling
+ 25 minutes cooking
FREEZING: recommended

FOR THE PASTRY:
175 g (6 oz) plain flour
80 g (3 oz) butter, diced
80 g (3 oz) icing sugar
3 egg yolks

FOR THE FILLING:
2 teaspoons gelatine
100 g (3½ oz) plain chocolate
1 teaspoon coffee granules
2 eggs, separated
50 g (2 oz) caster sugar
150 ml (5 fl oz) double cream,
    whipped to soft peaks

TO DECORATE:
150 ml (5 fl oz) double cream, whipped
chocolate-covered coffee beans

MOCHA TART

1   To make the pastry, place the flour, butter and icing sugar in a food processor and pulse until the mixture resembles breadcrumbs. Add the yolks and continue to process until a dough is formed. If you don't have a food processor, simply rub the butter into the flour and sugar and when the mixture resembles breadcrumbs, add the egg yolks and bring it all together to form a dough. Wrap the dough in clingfilm and chill for 30 minutes.

2   On a floured surface, roll out the pastry to fit a 20 cm (8-inch) loose-bottomed flan tin. Line the pastry case with baking parchment or foil and fill with baking beans. Chill for a further 20 minutes. Preheat the oven to Gas Mark 4/electric oven 180°C/fan oven 160°C. Bake the pastry case in the oven for 10 minutes, remove the parchment or foil and beans and bake for a further 10–15 minutes until the pastry is cooked and golden brown. Allow to cool on a wire rack.

3   In a small dish, sprinkle the gelatine over 30 ml (2 tablespoons) water and leave it to go spongy for 1 minute. Dissolve the gelatine by placing the dish in a larger one filled with hot water or by placing the dish in the microwave for 20 seconds. Stir the mixture to dissolve the gelatine completely and allow to cool.

4   Place the chocolate, coffee and 30 ml (2 tablespoons) water in a bowl and set it over a pan of barely simmering water, stirring from time to time until the chocolate melts. Remove the bowl from the heat and allow to cool. Stir in the egg yolks and sugar and mix thoroughly. Add the gelatine in a steady stream while mixing. Fold in the whipped cream.

5   Whisk the egg whites until they are stiff and fold in 1 tablespoon to loosen the chocolate mixture. Now add the remaining whites and fold them in using a figure-of-eight action until there are no whites visible. Pour the mixture into the pastry case, level the surface and chill until the mousse has set.

6   Place the whipped cream into a piping bag fitted with a star nozzle and pipe cream rosettes around the edge. Place a chocolate-covered coffee bean on each rosette.

SERVES 10–12
PREPARATION & COOKING TIME:
40 minutes + 2 hours chilling
+ 30 minutes cooking
FREEZING: recommended

This is a little time-consuming to prepare but well worth the effort. It **looks stunning** with the contrasting layers and would be an ideal buffet dessert. The raspberries are a perfect foil for the richness of the white chocolate mousse.

FOR THE PASTRY:
175 g (6 oz) plain flour
50 g (2 oz) cocoa powder
115 g (4 oz) unsalted butter, diced
115 g (4 oz) caster sugar
5 ml (1 teaspoon) vanilla extract
1 egg yolk

FOR THE FILLING:
2 tablespoons raspberry conserve
225 g (8 oz) fresh raspberries

FOR THE TOPPING:
2 teaspoons gelatine powder
200 g tub of cream cheese
200 g tub of crème fraîche
200 g tub of plain Greek yogurt
200 g (7 oz) white chocolate, melted

TO DECORATE:
cocoa powder
fresh raspberries

1. Sift the flour and cocoa into a large bowl and add the butter. Rub the butter into the flour until the mixture resembles breadcrumbs. Mix in the sugar. Add the vanilla extract, egg yolk and 15 ml (1 tablespoon) of cold water. Knead until the mixture comes together. You may need to add a little more water. Wrap in clingfilm and place in the fridge for an hour.
2. Allow the pastry to soften a little at room temperature. Sprinkle the work surface and rolling pin with a mixture of cocoa powder and icing sugar. Roll out the pastry so that it will fit a 25 cm (10-inch) loose-bottomed flan tin. Ease the pastry into the tin and with fingers dipped into the cocoa/icing sugar mixture, press the dough to fit the tin. Prick the pastry all over with a fork. You may need to use some trimmings to fit any gaps. Chill for a further hour.
3. Just before the hour is up, preheat the oven to Gas Mark 4/electric oven 180°C/fan oven 160°C. Line the pastry case with baking parchment or foil, fill with beans and bake in the oven for 15 minutes. Remove the paper or foil and beans and bake for a further 10 minutes until the pastry is cooked. Allow to cool in the tin on a wire rack.
4. When the pastry is cold, spread the base with raspberry conserve and scatter the raspberries on top.
5. To make the topping, sprinkle the gelatine over 30 ml (2 tablespoons) cold water in a dish and leave for a minute. Dissolve the gelatine by either placing the dish in a large bowl of hot water and stirring until it is dissolved or by microwaving on full power for 20 seconds. Cool.
6. Place the cream cheese, crème fraîche and yogurt in a bowl and beat together thoroughly. Fold in the melted white chocolate followed by the gelatine. Mix thoroughly and then spoon into the pastry case and spread the mousse so that there are no raspberries visible. Chill until set.
7. Just before serving, carefully remove the tart from the tin, lightly dust with sifted cocoa powder and pile some raspberries in the centre.

WHITE CHOCOLATE & RASPBERRY TART

SERVES 8
PREPARATION TIME: 25 minutes
FREEZING: recommended

Whenever I serve this dessert, I get asked for the recipe. It combines two hugely popular puddings and, for all **chocoholics**, it is heavenly. The cheesecake is very rich, so it is best to serve it in small slices.

FOR THE BASE:
80 g (3 oz) butter, melted
175 g (6 oz) digestive biscuits, crushed finely
50 g (2 oz) chopped and roasted hazelnuts

FOR THE FILLING:
175 g (6 oz) plain chocolate
225 g (8 oz) mascarpone, beaten
15 ml (1 tablespoon) strong black coffee, chilled
50 g (2 oz) caster sugar
150 ml (5 fl oz) whipping cream, whipped

FOR THE TOPPING:
225 g (8 oz) mascarpone
110 g (4 oz) plain Greek yogurt
cocoa powder
8–10 chocolate-coated coffee beans

1 Combine the melted butter, crushed biscuits and hazelnuts and press this into the base of a lightly greased 18 cm (7-inch) loose-bottomed cheesecake tin. Chill while you make the filling.

2 Melt the chocolate in a bowl set over a pan of simmering water and allow to cool a little. Place the mascarpone in a large bowl and fold in the coffee, sugar and melted chocolate, followed by the cream. Spoon the mixture into the tin and chill for a few hours until set.

3 To make the topping, combine the mascarpone and yogurt. Remove the cheesecake from the tin, and place it on a serving plate. Swirl the topping over the filling and dust with sifted cocoa powder. Decorate with the beans.

TIRAMISÙ CHEESECAKE

SERVES 8
PREPARATION & COOKING TIME:
30 minutes +1½ hours cooking
FREEZING: recommended

I have had a **love affair** with cheesecakes ever since my first taste of one in a restaurant on my 18th birthday – quite some time ago. There are endless varieties – this one should appeal to all chocoholics. The sweetness of the white chocolate offsets the more bitter flavour of the plain chocolate. Serving it warm really enhances the flavours. Accompany it with crème fraîche.

FOR THE BASE:
80 g (3 oz) butter, diced
1 tablespoon cocoa powder
225 g (8 oz) plain chocolate digestive biscuits, crushed into crumbs

FOR THE FILLING:
2 eggs, separated
80 g (3 oz) caster sugar
250 g carton of ricotta
50 g (2 oz) ground almonds
2 tablespoons Amaretto liqueur or brandy
150 ml (5 fl oz) double cream, whipped
80 g (3 oz) white chocolate, melted
25 g (1 oz) cocoa powder
cocoa powder and icing sugar, to decorate

1   Preheat the oven to Gas Mark 3/electric oven 170°C/fan oven 150°C. Lightly grease a 20 cm (8-inch) cheesecake tin or loose-bottomed cake tin.
2   Melt the butter and stir in the cocoa powder until it has dissolved. Add the crushed biscuits and mix thoroughly. Press the mixture down into the base of the tin and chill while you make the filling.
3   Whisk the egg yolks and sugar together until the mixture is thick and creamy. Add the ricotta, ground almonds and Amaretto or brandy. Mix gently until all the ingredients are incorporated. Fold in the whipped cream.
4   Add half the mixture to the cooled, melted white chocolate and stir the cocoa powder into the other half. Whisk the egg whites until they are stiff. Add a tablespoon to both bowls and beat in to loosen the mixtures. Divide the rest of the whites between the two bowls and fold in.
5   Spoon the white chocolate mixture on to the biscuit base leaving gaps for adding the dark chocolate mixture. Using a skewer, create a swirled effect with the two mixtures.
6   Bake in the oven for 1½ hours until the cheesecake is cooked. Leave in the tin for 10 minutes before transferring to a serving plate. Sift some cocoa powder over the top followed by a light sprinkling of icing sugar.

WARM WHITE & DARK CHOCOLATE CHEESECAKE

If I'm honest, I would have to admit that these are my favourite chocolate dishes – I would probably choose these to prepare at home or opt for in a restaurant. In this chapter, I have included recipes that will hopefully appeal to different age groups, such as Snickers Mousse for youngsters, and many that are quick to prepare, making allowances for our busy lifestyle.

COLD DESSERTS

There are also some desserts that are twists on more familiar versions, such as Chocolate Crème Caramel and Chocolate Brownie Ice Cream. What's more there are sauces here that can be served with many other desserts, for example, Dark Chocolate Sauce could be poured over Chocolate Brownie Ice Cream – a bit indulgent but deliciously decadent!

SERVES 6
PREPARATION TIME:
20 minutes + 2 hours soaking,
minimum + 3 hours chilling time
FREEZING: recommended

This is **scrummy** – chocolate, prunes and brandy make a heavenly combination! All this needs to accompany it is some chilled single cream. This is one of those desserts that is better sliced and put on plates in the kitchen before presenting to your guests.

BOOZY CHOCOLATE & PRUNE TERRINE

10 prunes, halved
40 ml (1¾ fl oz) brandy
225 g (8 oz) plain chocolate, broken into pieces
40 g (1½ oz) butter, cut into small pieces
300 ml (10 fl oz) double cream, whipped to soft peaks

TO SERVE:
single cream
cocoa powder

1 Place the prunes in a bowl, pour over the brandy and cover with clingfilm. Leave to soak for at least 2 hours – the longer the better.

2 Put the chocolate and 30 ml (2 tablespoons) water in a bowl over a pan of simmering water until the chocolate is melted. Remove the bowl from the heat and add the butter a little at a time, beating well – the chocolate will loosen and become very glossy. Allow to cool for a minute and then fold in the whipped cream carefully until it has all been incorporated. Stir in the prunes and the brandy.

3 Lightly oil a 450 g (1 lb) loaf tin and line with clingfilm. Spoon the chocolate mixture into the tin and level the surface. Place in the fridge for at least 3 hours.

4 To serve, turn out the terrine on to a board, cut into slices and place a slice on each serving plate. Pour some single cream around each slice and dust lightly with cocoa powder.

SERVES: 6–8
PREPARATION TIME: 20 minutes
FREEZING: not recommended

I'm not a fan of Christmas pudding, so each year I try to create **an alternative that includes chocolate!** This is quick to prepare using good quality convenience products – the inclusion of chocolate in the custard really complements the orange in the poached cranberries. I would like to dedicate this dessert to my friend, Karen, a fellow chocoholic who loves Green and Black's Maya Gold chocolate.

3 chocolate muffins, standard size
4 tablespoons cranberry sauce
115 g (4 oz) fresh cranberries
45 ml (3 tablespoons) fresh orange juice
190 g (6½ oz) caster sugar
500 g carton of custard
115 g (4 oz) Green and Black's Maya Gold chocolate, broken into pieces
150 ml (5 fl oz) ruby port
juice of 1 lemon
225 ml (8 fl oz) double cream
cocoa powder, to decorate

1 Split each muffin into three slices and spread each slice with cranberry sauce. Arrange in the base of a glass trifle bowl.
2 Place the cranberries, orange juice, 45 ml (3 tablespoons) water and 115 g (4 oz) of the caster sugar in a saucepan; bring to the boil and simmer gently until the cranberries are cooked. Strain the cranberries, reserving the poaching liquid, and spoon them over the muffins. Sprinkle 3 tablespoons of the reserved liquid over the cranberries and muffins.
3 Empty the custard into a saucepan and heat very gently until it is on the point of boiling. Remove from the heat, add the chocolate pieces and stir until the chocolate has melted. Allow to cool and then pour this mixture over the cranberries and chill while you prepare the syllabub.
4 Place the port, lemon juice and remaining sugar in a large bowl and stir until the sugar has dissolved. Add the cream and whisk, starting on a low speed, until the mixture has begun to thicken. Pour this over the trifle.
5 To decorate, cut out about seven stars from card and arrange lightly on the syllabub. Sift cocoa powder all over the surface and carefully lift the pieces of card from the top. Alternatively, you could simply dust the surface with sifted cocoa powder.

CHRISTMAS STAR TRIFLE

SERVES 6
PREPARATION TIME: 30 minutes + 30 minutes standing
FREEZING: not recommended

CHOCOLATE MOUSSE WITH ORANGE SYLLABUB

Chocolate and oranges go extremely well together and the slices of fresh oranges under the mousse are a perfect foil for the richness of the chocolate and the creamy syllabub.

110 g (4 oz) plain chocolate

3 oranges

300 ml (10 fl oz) double cream, whipped lightly

40 g (1½ oz) caster sugar

15 ml (1 tablespoon) Cointreau

grated chocolate, for decoration

1 Break the chocolate into pieces and place in a bowl with 30 ml (2 tablespoons) water over a pan of simmering water and allow to melt, stirring occasionally. Allow to cool.
2 Grate the zest from 2 oranges and add it to the chocolate. Fold in half the cream.
3 Peel both oranges and slice them. Divide the slices between six serving glasses. Spoon the chocolate mousse on top and refrigerate until set.
4 Combine the juice from the third orange with the sugar and Cointreau in a large bowl and leave for half an hour for the flavours to develop. Stir in the remaining cream and whisk until the mixture just holds its shape (it will continue to thicken in the fridge).
5 Spoon the syllabub on to the chocolate mousse and sprinkle over a little grated chocolate.

SERVES 6
PREPARATION TIME: 15 minutes + 2 hours freezing
FREEZING: essential

CHOCOLATE BROWNIE ICE CREAM

This is incredibly easy to make and far nicer than the equivalent found in the supermarkets. I made it using the Chocolate Brownies recipe (page 66), although you could use shop-bought brownies – but try and use the best you can get. It's delicious served with Dark Chocolate Sauce.

4 chocolate brownies

15 ml (1 tablespoon) bourbon or whisky

500 ml carton of real vanilla ice cream, softened a little

500 g carton of custard

Dark Chocolate Sauce (opposite), to serve

1 Break the brownies into pieces, taking care not to make too many crumbs. Sprinkle the bourbon or whisky over.
2 Place the ice cream and custard in a bowl and mix together quickly (you don't want the ice cream to melt). Fold in the brownie pieces and spoon the mixture into a tub and place in the freezer for a couple of hours.
3 Scoop into sundae dishes and pour some chocolate sauce over.

SERVES 4–6
PREPARATION TIME: 15 minutes + 2 hours freezing
FREEZING: essential

CHOCOLATE SORBET

This sorbet has an intensely rich chocolate flavour – it's hard to believe that it contains no cream! It would make an ideal dessert to serve at the end of a rich meal with a liqueur such as Tia Maria or crème de cacao poured over.

200 g (7 oz) caster sugar
25 g (1 oz) cocoa powder
600 ml (20 fl oz) water
80 g (3 oz) plain chocolate, broken into pieces
1 teaspoon vanilla extract
Tia Maria or crème de cacao, to serve (optional)

1   Place the sugar, cocoa powder and water in a saucepan and bring to the boil gradually, stirring, until the sugar has dissolved. Boil for 5 minutes, remove from the heat and add the chocolate pieces. Stir until the chocolate has melted. Add the vanilla extract and leave the mixture to cool completely.
2   Pour the mixture into a plastic tub with a lid and freeze for about 1 hour until the mixture has frozen. Remove the tub from the freezer and place the mixture into a food processor or blender and blend until smooth. Return the mixture straight away to the tub and place in the freezer for at least an hour or until it is required.
3   To serve, scoop out the sorbet into wine glasses or coffee cups and pour over some liqueur, if using.

     NOTE: The mixture can be churned in an ice cream maker, if you have one.

SERVES 6
PREPARATION TIME: 10 minutes
FREEZING: recommended

DARK CHOCOLATE SAUCE

Who can resist a rich, glossy, chocolate sauce? I just can't help myself dipping a finger into it when I think no-one is looking. You can vary the alcohol as you wish or simply replace it with orange juice if it's for children. This sauce is particularly good poured over ice cream.

80 g (3 oz) caster sugar
90 ml (6 tablespoons) water
150 g (5 oz) plain chocolate, broken into small pieces
25 g (1 oz) butter, diced
30 ml (2 tablespoons) brandy

1   Place the sugar and water in a saucepan and bring to the boil, stirring to dissolve the sugar.
2   Remove from the heat, add the chocolate and stir until it has melted.
3   Mix in the butter and continue to stir until the butter has melted. Add the brandy and blend it into the sauce.

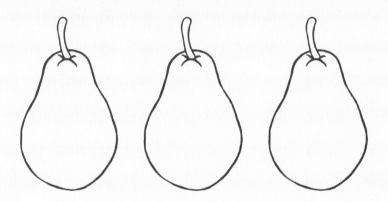

SERVES 4
PREPARATION & COOKING TIME:
20 minutes + 20 minutes cooking
FREEZING: not recommended

Pears with chocolate sauce is a classic French dessert. Stuffing the base of the pears with a crunchy nut filling adds an interesting taste and texture to the dish. Large ripe pears, such as Comice or William, are ideal for this **elegant dinner party dessert**.

30 ml (2 tablespoons) lemon juice
50 g (2 oz) caster sugar
300 ml (10 fl oz) water
1 cinnamon stick
4 ripe pears

FOR THE FILLING:
25 g (1 oz) chopped roasted hazelnuts
1 tablespoon light muscovado sugar
15 g (½ oz) butter, melted

FOR THE SAUCE:
50 g (2 oz) butter
115 g (4 oz) light muscovado sugar
1 tablespoon golden syrup
225 ml (8 fl oz) double cream
115 g (4 oz) plain chocolate,
broken into pieces

1 Place the lemon juice, caster sugar, water and cinnamon stick in a saucepan and heat gently to dissolve the sugar.
2 In the meantime, peel the pears carefully, leaving the stalk intact. Scoop out the cores from the base and create a hole for the filling. Place the pears in the syrup, turning them over to coat them. Bring to the boil, cover and simmer for 15–20 minutes or until they are tender. Remove the pears from the poaching liquid and allow to cool.
3 To make the filling, simple combine the ingredients together. When the pears have cooled, fill the cavities with the nut mixture and place each pear on a serving plate.
4 To make the sauce, place the butter, muscovado sugar and syrup in a saucepan and melt over a low heat. Add the cream and chocolate and bring to the boil, whisking continuously. Simmer for a minute over a low heat, cool a little and then pour the sauce over the top of the pears.

STUFFED PEARS WITH CHOCOLATE FUDGE SAUCE

SERVES 6–8
PREPARATION TIME: 30 minutes + 2 hours chilling
FREEZING: recommended

CHOCOLATE ORANGE BOMBE

Green and Black's Maya Gold chocolate is ideal for this recipe as it is tinged with an orange flavour. Alternatively, you could use plain chocolate and add the grated zest of two oranges when you add the ricotta. Served with a clementine compote, **this would make a perfect alternative to Christmas pudding**.

100 g bar of Maya Gold chocolate
80 g (3 oz) unsalted butter, diced
I sachet gelatine
150 ml (5 fl oz) fresh orange juice
250 g tub of ricotta
50 g (2 oz) blanched almonds, halved
about 24 sponge fingers
300 ml (20 fl oz) whipping cream, whipped to soft peaks

TO DECORATE:
clementine segments
toasted flaked almonds

1   Place the chocolate and butter in a bowl and set it over a pan of barely simmering water. Stir occasionally until the chocolate and butter have melted. Remove from the heat, stir thoroughly and allow to cool.

2   Sprinkle the gelatine over the orange juice in a small dish or cup and leave for a minute. Dissolve the gelatine either by placing the dish or cup in a large bowl of hot water or by heating it in the microwave for 40 seconds on full power. Stir well and allow to cool.

3   Add the ricotta and the almonds to the chocolate mixture and mix well. Place three sponge fingers in the base of a 1.2-litre (2-pint) pudding basin, sugar side down. Spread some of the chocolate mixture on top using a small spatula. Place four sponge fingers on top at cross angles to the first three. Add a layer of the chocolate mixture and continue to layer, finishing with sponge fingers.

4   Using a skewer, pierce the mixture several times and then pour over the orange gelatine mixture, easing the sponge mixture away from the sides so that the juices reach the bottom. Cover with clingfilm and place in the fridge for 2 hours to set.

5   Dip the blade of a knife in hot water and then run it around the sides of the bowl. Dip the bowl in a larger bowl of hot water for a minute and then turn it out on to a serving plate.

6   Spread two-thirds of the cream all over the bombe and place the remaining cream in a piping bag and pipe cream around the bottom (alternatively simply spread all the cream over the bombe). Decorate with clementine segments and scatter toasted almonds all over the cream.

SERVES 6
PREPARATION TIME: 20 minutes
FREEZING: not recommended

SNICKERS MOUSSE

All fans of this chocolate bar should love this mousse – my daughter, Holly, certainly does! If you love peanuts, you could add some extra. The cocoa powder used here is just enough to bring out the chocolate flavour without overpowering the caramel.

64.5 g bar of Snickers chocolate
300 ml (10 fl oz) double cream
1 tablespoon cocoa powder
200 g (7 oz) cream cheese

TO DECORATE:
chopped peanuts
grated chocolate or sifted cocoa powder

1 Chop the bar of Snickers chocolate and place it in a bowl with half the cream and the cocoa. Place the bowl over a pan of barely simmering hot water, stirring from time to time until the chocolate bar has melted and the ingredients are blended together.
2 Remove the bowl from the pan and allow the mixture to cool. Whip the remaining cream until it reaches the soft peak stage. Beat the cream cheese into the chocolate mix and then fold in the whipped cream until it is thoroughly incorporated.
3 Spoon the mousse into glass dishes or ramekin dishes and decorate with peanuts, grated chocolate or cocoa powder.

SERVES 8
PREPARATION TIME: 30 MINUTES
FREEZING: not recommended

ITALIAN MOCHA TRIFLE

A short while ago I offered to take a pudding to a friend's house for a dinner party and created this trifle from my store cupboard ingredients. I am pleased to say that it was a huge success.

80 g (3 oz) sponge fingers, halved
125 g (4½ oz) amaretti biscuits
90 ml (5 tablespoons) sherry
2 tablespoons custard powder
2 tablespoons cocoa powder
2 teaspoons coffee granules
2 heaped tablespoons soft brown sugar
600 ml (20 fl oz) milk
3 bananas
300 ml (10 fl oz) double cream, whipped
chocolate shavings, to decorate

1 Place the sponge fingers and amaretti biscuits in the base of a large glass dish and sprinkle the sherry over.
2 Place the custard powder, cocoa, coffee and sugar in a bowl and stir in a little of the milk to form a paste. Heat the rest of the milk in a medium saucepan until it is nearly boiling and then add to the paste, stirring all the time to avoid any lumps appearing in the sauce. Return the sauce to the pan and bring to the boil, stirring all the time. Allow to cool.
3 Slice the bananas and arrange them on top of the biscuit mixture. Pour the cooled mocha custard on top making sure that all the bananas are covered.
4 Spread the cream on top and decorate with the chocolate shavings (make these by pulling a vegetable peeler along the edge of a bar of chocolate).

SERVES 6
PREPARATION TIME: 5–10 minutes
FREEZING: not recommended

It's wonderful to have a simple, **sophisticated** dessert up your sleeve when you're either very busy or have unexpected guests. This fits the bill perfectly. You'll have guests guessing how you made the sauce! I find it best to thaw the fruits in a single layer on a plate lined with kitchen paper.

500 g bag of frozen summer fruits, defrosted
150 g (5½ oz) white chocolate,
broken into pieces
300 ml (10 fl oz) sour cream

1 Divide the fruit between six wine glasses or sundae dishes.
2 Melt the chocolate by placing it in a bowl set over a pan of barely simmering hot water, stirring from time to time. Remove from the heat and allow to cool.
3 Stir a spoonful of the cream into the melted chocolate and mix well. Add the remaining cream and mix thoroughly. Spoon over the fruit and serve.

SUMMER FRUITS WITH WHITE CHOCOLATE SAUCE

SERVES 4–6
PREPARATION & COOKING TIME:
20 minutes + 50–60 minutes cooking
FREEZING: not recommended

Chocolate and caramel go very well together, so it seems only natural that the addition of chocolate to this **traditional favourite** would create a delicious dessert. Serve this with some single cream.

CHOCOLATE CRÈME CARAMEL

115 g (4 oz) granulated sugar
115 ml (4 fl oz) water
300 ml (10 fl oz) single cream
300 ml (10 fl oz) milk
115 g (4 oz) plain chocolate, broken into pieces
3 eggs
2 egg yolks
2.5 ml (½ teaspoon) vanilla extract
50 g (2 oz) caster sugar

1 Preheat the oven to Gas Mark 2/electric oven 150°C/fan oven 130°C. Lightly butter a deep baking dish, such as a soufflé dish.

2 Place the granulated sugar and water in a heavy-based saucepan and stir to dissolve the sugar. Bring to the boil and boil without stirring, until the mixture turns a caramel colour. Pour it straight away into the prepared dish and swirl it around to cover the bottom of the dish.

3 Place the cream and milk in another saucepan and heat until nearly boiling. Add the chocolate and stir until it has melted completely. Place the eggs, egg yolks, vanilla extract and caster sugar in a large bowl and whisk together. Pour the chocolate mixture on top and whisk to incorporate all the ingredients. Pour this on to the caramel through a sieve and place the dish into a roasting tin half-filled with hot water.

4 Bake in the oven for 50–60 minutes until the custard is set. Remove from the roasting tin and allow to cool. Chill for at least two hours before serving.

This is a chapter of classic recipes. I have given a makeover to a couple, so the Roulade has a tiramisù filling and the Crème Brûlée has a chocolate custard. Profiteroles with Chocolate Sauce must be one of the most popular and enduring dessert on any menu – I hope you like my version! Zuccotto is probably the least well known, but is a perfect

CONTINENTAL CHOCOLATE CLASSICS

finale to any Italian meal. Although many recipes in this chapter are wonderfully elegant and sophisticated, there are some informal dishes as well, such as Chocolate Fondue, for a messy but fun occasion.

SERVES 6

PREPARATION TIME: 30 minutes

FREEZING: not recommended

These little mousses are a **chocolate lover's dream** – they have such an intense smooth chocolate flavour. Served in demi-tasse coffee cups, these make an elegant end to a special dinner.

300 ml (10 fl oz) double cream
115 ml (4 fl oz) milk
50 g (2 oz) icing sugar
4 egg yolks, whisked
200 g (7 oz) plain chocolate,
broken into pieces
15 ml (1 tablespoon) brandy
single cream, to serve

1 Place the cream and milk in a saucepan, add the icing sugar and stir to dissolve while bringing the mixture to the boil.
2 Pour this mixture on to the egg yolks, while whisking, to create a thin custard. Pour the custard through a sieve into a clean bowl, and cover with clingfilm. Let it cool to room temperature.
3 Place the chocolate in a bowl and set it over a pan of barely simmering hot water. Remove from the heat and allow it to cool a little.
4 Pour the custard gradually on to the chocolate while whisking. Add the brandy and mix thoroughly. Spoon or pour into six demi-tasse cups, cover with clingfilm and chill.
5 Just before serving, pour some single cream on top.

PETIT POTS AU CHOCOLAT

SERVES 8
PREPARATION & COOKING TIME:
30–40 minutes + 45–50 minutes cooking
FREEZING: recommended

SACHERTORTE

This famous Austrian chocolate gâteau was created by Franz Sacher in 1832. A friend of mine, Kay, visited the famous Sacher Café in Vienna and was disappointed with the sachertorte as it was very dry. I was therefore keen to produce one that was moist and I am pleased to say that Kay gave my version the thumbs up. It is very rich, so small slices are advisable.

FOR THE CAKE:

225 g (8 oz) plain chocolate, broken into pieces
175 g (6 oz) unsalted butter, softened
150 g (5 oz) caster sugar
5 ml (1 teaspoon) vanilla extract
5 eggs, separated
80 g (3 oz) ground almonds
50 g (2 oz) plain flour

FOR THE FILLING AND ICING:

8 tablespoons apricot jam
15 ml (1 tablespoon) lemon juice
30 ml (2 tablespoons) whisky
175 g (6 oz) plain chocolate, broken into pieces
80 g (3 oz) butter, cut into small dice
80 g (3 oz) double cream
50 g (2 oz) milk chocolate, broken into pieces

1   Preheat the oven to Gas Mark 4/electric oven 180°C/fan oven 160°C. Grease and line the base of a 20 cm (8-inch) cake tin with baking parchment.

2   Melt the chocolate by placing it in a bowl and set it over a pan of barely simmering hot water. Stir and allow to cool. Meanwhile, whisk the butter and sugar in another bowl until the mixture is light and creamy. Beat in the vanilla extract followed by the egg yolks, one at a time. Add the ground almonds and flour and mix in thoroughly. Whisk the egg whites until they are stiff in a large spotlessly clean bowl. Add a large spoonful to the chocolate mixture and beat in to loosen the mixture. Add the remaining whites and fold them in gently using a figure-of-eight action.

3   Spoon the mixture into the prepared tin, level the surface and bake for 45–50 minutes until the cake has risen and is firm to the touch. Allow to cool for a few minutes in the tin, and then turn out and cool completely on a wire rack.

4   Heat the apricot jam with the lemon juice and sieve it. Cut the cake in half horizontally. Sprinkle the whisky over the cut surfaces. Place the bottom half on a plate and spread the cut surface with a third of the jam mixture. Place the other cake half on top. Spread the remaining jam all over the top and sides of the cake and then leave it to set

5   Melt the plain chocolate as in Step 2. Remove the bowl from the heat and stir in the butter until it has melted. Stir in the cream and leave the sauce to thicken a little so that it will spread easily. Pour the chocolate icing on to the cake and spread it evenly all over. Leave it to set.

6   Melt the milk chocolate as in Step 2. Spoon it into a small disposable piping bag or plastic food bag and snip off a small corner. Pipe the name 'Sacher' across the top and, once again, leave to set.

SERVES 4
PREPARATION & COOKING TIME:
40 minutes + 25 minutes cooking
FREEZING: recommended – unfilled choux
buns and chocolate sauce should ideally be frozen separately

PROFITEROLES WITH CHOCOLATE SAUCE

These little choux buns filled with cream and covered in a rich, dark chocolate sauce have been a long-time favourite of mine. They look so impressive when piled high into a pyramid on a large platter. Choux pastry is easier than most people imagine – just weigh the ingredients accurately and follow the method to the letter. If you make the choux buns in advance, it's best to crisp them up in a warm oven just before filling with the cream.

FOR THE CHOUX PASTRY:
150 ml (5 fl oz) water
50 g (2 oz) butter, cubed
50 g (2 oz) plus 2 tablespoons plain flour, sifted
a pinch of salt
2 eggs, beaten

FOR THE FILLING:
300 ml (10 fl oz) whipping cream
5 ml (1 teaspoon) vanilla extract

FOR THE SAUCE:
150 ml (5 fl oz) double cream
80 g (3 oz) butter, cubed
25 g (1 oz) light muscovado sugar
1 tablespoon golden syrup
115 g (4 oz) plain chocolate, broken into pieces

1 Preheat the oven to Gas Mark 4/electric oven 180°C/fan oven 160°C. Place the water and butter in a saucepan and heat gently until the butter has melted. Remove from the heat and immediately add the flour, with the salt, all at once, stirring it into the liquid thoroughly. Using a wooden spoon, beat the eggs into the mixture, a little at a time, beating well between each addition – the mixture should come away from the sides of the pan and look glossy.

2 Line a baking sheet with baking parchment. Fill a piping bag with the pastry mixture and pipe 16 small mounds on to the baking sheet. Bake in the oven for 10 minutes and then increase the temperature to Gas Mark 5/electric oven 190°C/fan oven 170°C and bake for a further 10 minutes. Increase the temperature again to Gas Mark 6/electric oven 200°C/fan oven 180°C and bake for 5 minutes more, until the buns are golden brown and crisp.

3 Make a small slit in the side of each bun and place them on a wire rack to cool. While they are cooling, make the filling. Whip the cream with the vanilla extract to form soft peaks. Fill a piping bag with the cream and fill the buns with vanilla-flavoured cream through the slit. Arrange on a serving platter, ideally piled into a pyramid.

4 To make the sauce, place the cream, butter, muscovado sugar and syrup in a medium saucepan. Heat over a low heat until the butter has melted and the sugar has dissolved. Remove from the heat , add the chocolate and stir until it has melted – the sauce should be smooth and glossy. Pour some of the sauce over the profiteroles and serve the remainder separately in a jug.

SERVES 6
PREPARATION TIME:
30 minutes + 2 hours chilling
FREEZING: recommended

**2 x 18 cm (7-inch) round chocolate
sponge cakes (see Quick Chocolate
Cake, page 19)
80 g (3 oz) plain chocolate
60 ml (4 tablespoons) Amaretto
60 ml (4 tablespoons) brandy
or orange juice
425 ml (¾ pint) double cream
80 g (3 oz) unblanched almonds,
chopped
80 g (3 oz) chopped hazelnuts
115 g (4 oz) glacé cherries, halved
2 tablespoons icing sugar
80 g (3 oz) plain chocolate, chopped
icing sugar and cocoa powder,
to decorate**

This famous Italian bombe gets its name from its shape which resembles a pumpkin – **'zucca'**. There are many interpretations: some use Madeira cake for the casing, others use sponge fingers, and the filling varies. I hope you like my recipe which uses the Quick Chocolate Cake for its shell.

1   Lightly oil a 1.25-litre (2-pint) pudding basin and line it with clingfilm.
2   Cut each sponge cake in half horizontally. Use three of the sponge pieces to line the sides and base of a pudding basin, cutting and trimming where necessary, making sure there are no gaps.
3   Melt the chocolate in a bowl over a pan of barely simmering water and then leave to cool. Mix the Amaretto and the brandy or orange juice in a jug and sprinkle about two-thirds over the sponge shell. Whip the cream so it is fairly stiff.
4   Add the almonds, hazelnuts, cherries, icing sugar and chopped chocolate to the cream. Fold in the cooled, melted chocolate and spoon the mixture into the cavity. Cut a circle from the fourth piece of sponge large enough to cover the filling. Place it on the filling, making sure there are no gaps, and sprinkle with the remaining alcohol mixture. Cover with clingfilm and chill for at least 2 hours.
5   Turn out the zuccotto on to a serving plate, first removing the clingfilm. Dust it all over with sifted icing sugar and then sift a little cocoa powder on top of the bombe. Serve cut into wedges.

ZUCCOTTO

SERVES 6
PREPARATION TIME:
25 minutes + 2 hours chilling
FREEZING: not recommended

50 g (2 oz) caster sugar
4 egg yolks
1 heaped teaspoon cornflour
1 tablespoon cocoa powder
300 ml (10 fl oz) double cream
300 ml (10 fl oz) milk
100 g bar of plain chocolate,
broken into squares
6 teaspoons icing sugar, sifted

My version of this universally **popular dessert** has the advantage of not requiring any baking. If you don't possess a blowtorch, place the ramekins in a roasting tin with enough cold water to come two-thirds up the sides of the dishes – this prevents the chocolate custards from getting hot and cooking while under the grill. I would recommend eating this with a teaspoon to make it last longer!

1 Put the caster sugar, egg yolks, cornflour and cocoa powder in a bowl and mix well.
2 Place the cream and milk in a medium saucepan and gently bring to the boil. Pour this on to the egg mixture, whisking continuously. Return the mixture to the pan and heat gently, stirring, until it has thickened.
3 Remove the pan from the heat and stir in the chocolate pieces until they have melted. Pour the mixture into six ramekin dishes and allow to cool before placing in the fridge to chill for a couple of hours.
4 Sprinkle the surfaces evenly with the icing sugar and caramelise the top either by using a blowtorch or placing under a hot preheated grill. Chill for at least 2 hours, or until ready to serve.

CHOCOLATE CRÈME BRÛLÉE

SERVES 6–8
PREPARATION & COOKING TIME:
30 minutes + 20 minutes cooking
+ 2 hours standing
FREEZING: recommended

This recipe combines two of my favourite desserts!

Don't be put off by making a roulade – it isn't as difficult as you might imagine. I find that covering the cooked mixture with a damp tea towel for at least a couple of hours before rolling it up really helps.

175 g (6 oz) plain chocolate,
broken into pieces
5 eggs, separated
175 g (6 oz) caster sugar
icing sugar, for dusting
250 g tub of mascarpone
150 ml (5 fl oz) whipping cream,
whipped to soft peaks
50 g (2 oz) chocolate-covered coffee beans

1 Preheat the oven to Gas Mark 4/electric oven 180°C/fan oven 160°C. Grease and line a 35 cm x 25 cm (14-inch x 10-inch) swiss roll tin with baking parchment.

2 Melt the chocolate by placing it in a bowl set over a pan of barely simmering water. Remove from the heat.

3 Meanwhile, place the egg yolks and sugar in another bowl and whisk until pale and creamy. Wash the whisks thoroughly and whisk the egg whites in another bowl until they are stiff.

4 Whisk or beat the melted chocolate into the egg yolk mixture. Spoon a little of the egg whites into the chocolate mixture and beat in to loosen it. Using a large metal spoon, fold in the remaining whites carefully using a figure-of-eight action until there are no whites visible.

5 Pour the mixture into the prepared tin and gently spread it to the corners. Bake for 15–20 minutes, until the roulade has risen and is firm to the touch. Place a cooling rack to balance on the edges of the tin and then place a damp tea towel on top to cover the whole roulade (the wire rack should not touch the roulade). Leave for at least 2 hours.

6 Cut a piece of greaseproof paper larger than the roulade and dust liberally with sifted icing sugar. Turn out the roulade on to the paper. Empty the mascarpone cheese into a mixing bowl and beat to soften it. Fold in the whipped cream and spread the mixture all over the surface of the roulade but not right up to the edges. Scatter the chocolate coffee beans over the cream.

7 Position the roulade so that a short side is facing you. Hold the edge of the paper and use it to roll up the roulade. Slide it on to a serving plate with the seam underneath and dust with a little more icing sugar.

TIRAMISÙ ROULADE

The smell of a chocolate pudding baking in the oven is irresistible and always makes me feel hungry. Once again, I have adapted familiar puddings to incorporate chocolate, for example White Chocolate Bread and Butter Pudding and Chocolate Meringue Pie. The

HOT PUDDINGS

Little Chocolate Puddings and Hot Chocolate Soufflé have been devised to allow for the bulk of the preparation to be done in advance. The Rhubarb, Ginger and White Chocolate Crumble sounds a little unusual but the flavours work really well together.

SERVES 4
PREPARATION & COOKING TIME:
20 minutes + 40–50 minutes cooking
FREEZING: recommended

These ingredients go so very well together. If you are a real fan of ginger, you could add a teaspoon of powdered ginger to the crumble mixture. **Serve with lashings of hot custard or thick cream!** If you cannot get young, tender rhubarb, you will need to poach the rhubarb a little before adding the crumble.

RHUBARB, GINGER & WHITE CHOCOLATE CRUMBLE

FOR THE CRUMBLE:
100 g (3½ oz) plain flour
50 g (2 oz) porridge oats
65 g (2½ oz) butter, diced
50 g (2 oz) caster sugar
80 g (3 oz) white chocolate pieces

FOR THE FILLING:
675 g (1½ lb) young rhubarb, cut into small slices
80 g (3 oz) soft brown sugar
2 pieces stem ginger, diced finely

1 Preheat the oven to Gas Mark 4/electric oven 180°C/fan oven 160°C.
2 Place the flour and oats in a bowl with the butter and rub in the butter until the mixture resembles rough breadcrumbs. Stir in the sugar and white chocolate pieces.
3 Butter an ovenproof dish and fill with the rhubarb pieces. Spread them out evenly and scatter over the sugar and ginger. Spoon the crumble over the rhubarb, making sure that there is no fruit visible. Bake in the oven for 40–45 minutes until the crumble is cooked and golden brown.

SERVES 4
PREPARATION TIME & COOKING TIME: 30 minutes
FREEZING: recommended – crêpes only

CHOCOLATE CRÊPES WITH BANANA RUM CREAM

I would recommend that you use a crêpe pan to make the crêpes – the results will be far better. If you are short of time or are not confident about making the crêpes, you could cheat by buying ready-made ones and spreading the inside of each one with a good quality chocolate spread. The rum can be replaced with vanilla extract for children. If you are feeling really indulgent, you could serve the crêpes with some chocolate fudge sauce (see page 38) poured over them.

FOR THE CRÊPES:
90 g (3¼ oz) plain flour
2 tablespoons cocoa powder
1 tablespoon icing sugar
1 egg
1 teaspoon sunflower oil
300 ml (10 fl oz) milk
butter, for frying

FOR THE FILLING:
300 ml (10 fl oz) whipping cream
1 tablespoon icing sugar
15 ml (1 tablespoon) rum
2 bananas

1 To make the crêpes, sift the flour, cocoa and icing sugar into a bowl. Make a well in the middle and place the egg and oil in it. Using a whisk, bring the mixture together to form a smooth batter by adding the milk a little at a time.

2 Put a knob of butter in a crêpe pan and when it has melted, ladle some batter into the pan. Swirl it around to cover the base and cook until the underside is light golden. Turn over and cook the other side. Repeat until all the mixture has been used, layering the pancakes on a plate with a circle of greaseproof paper separating each pancake. Cover with foil and keep warm while you prepare the filling.

3 Whip the cream with the icing sugar and rum to form soft peaks. Slice the bananas at a slight angle. Divide them between the crêpes and either roll them up or fold in half and in half again to form triangles. Place the crêpes on serving plates and spoon the rum cream alongside them.

SERVES 6
PREPARATION & COOKING TIME: 30 minutes +
1 hour freezing + 25 minutes cooking
FREEZING: not recommended

LITTLE CHOCOLATE PUDDINGS

These puddings, like soufflés, need to be eaten as soon as they come out of the oven. However, not many people would contemplate preparing them in the middle of a dinner party. I am pleased to say that most of the preparation can be done a couple of hours in advance and then finished off just before popping them in the oven. The ganache in the middle of the puddings turns into a delicious chocolate sauce when cooked. Serve with plenty of pouring cream.

FOR THE CHOCOLATE GANACHE:
65 ml (2½ fl oz) double cream
65 g (2½ oz) plain chocolate, broken into pieces
15 ml (1 tablespoon) brandy

FOR THE PUDDINGS:
100 g (3½ oz) plain chocolate, broken into pieces
175 g (6 oz) unsalted butter, softened
150 g (5 oz) caster sugar
3 eggs, beaten
225 g (8 oz) self-raising flour
25 g (1 oz) cocoa powder
a pinch of salt
60 ml (4 tablespoons) milk

1 To make the chocolate ganache, heat the cream in a saucepan until it is about to boil. Remove it from the heat and add the chocolate pieces. Stir the chocolate until it has melted and then stir in the brandy. Allow the ganache to cool. Line a small square container with clingfilm, pour in the ganache, cover and then freeze for at least 1 hour or until you are ready to bake the puddings.

2 Preheat the oven to Gas Mark 4/electric oven 180°C/fan oven 160°C. Grease and line the base of six individual pudding basins or ramekin dishes.

3 To make the puddings, melt the chocolate over a pan of barely simmering water and set aside to cool. Place the butter and sugar in a bowl and whisk or beat until the mixture is creamy and light. Add the eggs, a little at a time, beating well between each addition. Sift the flour and cocoa powder together and add this to the mixture with the salt – at this point the mixture will seem a little dry. Add the milk followed by the melted chocolate. Spoon the mixture into the prepared dishes.

4 When you are ready to bake the puddings, remove the ganache from the freezer, turn it out on to a chopping board and cut it into six equal pieces. Place a piece in the middle of each pudding and press it down into the middle making sure there is no ganache visible.

5 Place the dishes in a roasting tin, half-filled with hot water, and bake for 25 minutes or until they have risen and are firm to the touch. Remove the containers from the tin and allow to cool for a couple of minutes. Run a knife around the edges to loosen the puddings and invert on to the palm of your hand. Place each pudding in the centre of a plate. Serve straightaway.

SERVES 6
PREPARATION & COOKING TIME:
20 minutes + 2¼ hours cooking
FREEZING: recommended

If you like steamed puddings, you will love this.

The addition of the dates to the chocolate mixture makes

it extra moist and the nuts give it a nice crunch.

80 g (3 oz) soft margarine
150 g (5 oz) light muscovado sugar
2 eggs
150 g (5 oz) self-raising flour, sieved
25 g (1 oz) cocoa powder, sifted
½ teaspoon bicarbonate of soda
115 g (4 oz) dates, cut into small pieces
115 g (4 oz) milk chocolate,
cut into small pieces
50 g (2 oz) walnut pieces

FOR THE SAUCE:
500 g carton of custard
115 g (4 oz) white chocolate

1 Grease a 1.2-litre (2-pint) pudding basin and place two wide strips of greaseproof paper in a cross, long enough to slightly overlap the rim.
2 Place the margarine, sugar, eggs, flour, cocoa and bicarbonate of soda in a mixing bowl and beat together until the mixture is creamy. Add the remaining ingredients and mix well. Spoon into the prepared basin and level the surface. Place two circles of greaseproof paper on top, followed by a large piece of foil with a pleat in the middle. Tuck the foil under the rim of the basin so that it fits snugly.
3 Half fill a large saucepan with boiling water and carefully lower the basin into the pan. Cover with the lid and steam for 2¼ hours. Check the water level from time to time and top up with boiling water, as necessary.
4 To make the sauce, place the custard and white chocolate in a saucepan and, over a very gentle heat, stir the sauce until the chocolate has melted.
5 To serve, remove the paper and foil from the top of the basin and turn out the pudding on to a large serving dish (the greaseproof paper strips help with this). Pour some of the sauce over the top and serve the remainder in a jug.

CHOCOLATE & DATE PUDDING WITH WHITE CHOCOLATE SAUCE

CHOCOLATE FONDUE

SERVES 4
PREPARATION & COOKING TIME: 10 minutes
FREEZING: recommended

My friend, Wendy, bought me a chocolate fondue set for a Christmas present a few years ago and it has been well used. Chocolate fondues are perfect to serve at the end of an informal meal, as I often do with a group of girlfriends. Napkins or bibs are essential as it can get quite messy.

80 g (3 oz) light or dark muscovado sugar
300 ml (10 fl oz) double cream
a squeeze of lemon juice
115 g (4 oz) plain chocolate, broken into pieces
15 ml (1 tablespoon) brandy

TO SERVE:
a selection of fruit (strawberries, bananas, pears, physalis, kiwi)
marshmallows

1 Place the sugar, cream and lemon juice in a heavy-based saucepan and bring to the boil over a gentle heat. Stir from time to time to dissolve the sugar.
2 Remove from the heat, add the chocolate and stir until it has melted. Stir in the brandy.
3 Place the fondue mixture in a bowl and set in the middle of a large platter.
4 Arrange the prepared fruit and marshmallows in an attractive pattern around the bowl and serve.

BAKED CHOCOLATE RASPBERRY PUDDING

SERVES 4–6
PREPARATION & COOKING TIME:
10 minutes + 45 minutes cooking
FREEZING: not recommended

White chocolate and raspberries are such wonderful partners. This is a simple yet delicious way of combining these flavours. It can be served cold, but I think this is much better served hot or warm with some single cream poured over.

450 g (1 lb) fresh raspberries
1 tablespoon caster sugar
30 ml (2 tablespoons) kirsch (optional)
225 g (8 oz) plain Greek yogurt
2 eggs
1 tablespoon plain flour
50 g (2 oz) white chocolate, chopped finely

1 Preheat the oven to Gas Mark 2/electric oven 150°C/fan oven 130°C. Lightly grease a shallow gratin dish.
2 Place the raspberries in an even layer in the dish and sprinkle over the sugar and the kirsch, if using. Place the yogurt, eggs and flour in a bowl and whisk together. Fold in the white chocolate pieces and spoon over the raspberries making sure that there are no raspberries visible.
3 Bake in the oven for 40–45 minutes until the topping is firm and set (at this point, some raspberries and their juices will probably be peeping through). Spoon into dishes.

SERVES 4–6
PREPARATION & COOKING TIME:
20 minutes + 40 minutes cooking
FREEZING: recommended

MAGIC CHOCOLATE PUDDING

This pudding is so called because a sauce is '**magically**' created while it cooks. White chocolate pieces in the bottom of the pudding creates a creamy chocolate sauce and the almonds provide a lovely crunch to the sponge. It's also called 'magic' as it disappears before your eyes as soon you put it on the table. Serve with some chilled single cream.

115 g (4 oz) soft margarine or butter
115 g (4 oz) caster sugar
2 eggs, beaten lightly
2 tablespoons cocoa powder
80 g (3 oz) self-raising flour
a pinch of salt
25 g (1 oz) flaked almonds
5 ml (1 teaspoon) vanilla extract
a little milk
50 g (2 oz) white chocolate, broken into small pieces

FOR THE SAUCE:
2 tablespoons cocoa
115 g (4 oz) muscovado sugar, preferably dark
300 ml (10 fl oz) boiling water

1 Preheat the oven to Gas Mark 5/electric oven 190°C/fan oven 170°C. Grease a 1.2-litre (2-pint) soufflé dish.
2 Cream the margarine or butter with the sugar until it is light and fluffy. Gradually add the beaten eggs. Sift the cocoa, flour and salt and add to the mixture with the flaked almonds. Add the vanilla extract with enough milk so that the mixture is of a 'dropping' consistency.
3 Scatter the white chocolate pieces evenly on the bottom of the prepared dish and spoon the mixture on top.
4 Make the sauce by dissolving the cocoa and sugar in the boiling water. Pour this over the sponge mixture and bake in the oven for 40 minutes until the pudding is risen and the top is firm to the touch.

SERVES 6
PREPARATION & COOKING TIME:
20 minutes + 30 minutes cooking
FREEZING: not recommended

This cheat's version of lemon meringue pie would be ideal for a family meal such as Sunday lunch – it is quick to prepare and will appeal to all age groups. You could add some chocolate chips to the chocolate filling to add a delicious crunch to it. Serve with some chilled single cream.

3 tablespoons custard powder
3 tablespoons caster sugar
425 ml (¾ pint) milk
100 g (3½ oz) plain chocolate, broken into squares
1 sweet pastry case
2 egg whites
100 g (3½ oz) caster sugar

1   Preheat the oven to Gas Mark 3/electric oven 170°C/fan oven 150°C.
2   To make the filling, place the custard powder and sugar in a bowl. Mix to a paste with a little of the milk. Heat the remaining milk until almost boiling. Using a whisk, add it to the custard paste. Return the custard mixture to the saucepan and heat gently, stirring continuously, until it thickens. Remove the pan from the heat, add the chocolate pieces and stir until the chocolate has melted. Spoon the mixture into the pastry case.
3   To make the meringue, whisk the egg whites until they are fairly stiff and then add the sugar a little at a time while still whisking. Pipe or spread the meringue over the chocolate filling (if you have done the latter, use a knife to create peaks in the meringue).
4   Bake in the oven for 30 minutes or until the meringue is golden brown. Serve cut into wedges with some cream poured over each slice.

CHOCOLATE MERINGUE PIE

SERVES 4
PREPARATION & COOKING TIME:
20 minutes + 40 minutes cooking
FREEZING: not recommended

I prepared this soufflé when a friend came to stay. Knowing time would be at a premium, I wanted to prepare most of the soufflé in advance and simply fold in the egg whites just before dinner. **It worked like a dream!** For a dinner party, you could prepare most of the soufflé in the afternoon, as I did, and finish it just before you sit down to eat the main course. It tastes delicious **and looks so impressive!** Serve with cream or real vanilla ice cream.

15 g (½ oz) butter
150 ml (5 fl oz) single cream
150 ml (5 fl oz) milk
4 eggs, separated
50 g (2 oz) caster sugar
1 tablespoon cornflour
100 g (3½ oz) plain chocolate,
broken into pieces
icing sugar, for dusting

1 Place the butter, cream and milk in a saucepan and place over a moderate heat.
2 Meanwhile, whisk the egg yolks and sugar together until the mixture is pale and creamy. Stir in the cornflour and mix until it is blended. Pour on the hot, creamy milk and whisk until smooth. Return the mixture to the saucepan and heat until it thickens, stirring often. Remove it from the heat, add the chocolate and stir until it has melted. At this stage, you can set the mixture aside until you are ready to put it in the oven.
3 Preheat the oven to Gas Mark 5/electric oven 190°C/fan oven 170°C. Grease an 18 cm (7-inch) soufflé dish and dust with caster sugar.
4 Whisk the egg whites in a large, clean bowl until they are stiff. Place a large spoonful of the whites in the chocolate mixture and beat in to loosen. Add the remaining whites and fold in carefully with a metal spoon, using a figure-of-eight action.
5 Spoon the chocolate mixture into the prepared soufflé dish and bake in the oven for 35–40 minutes until the soufflé has risen and has a slight wobble – if it is very wobbly, it needs a few more minutes in the oven. Dust with some icing sugar and serve.

HOT CHOCOLATE SOUFFLÉ

SERVES 6
PREPARATION & COOKING TIME:
20 minutes + 2 hours chilling
+ 35 minutes cooking
FREEZING: not recommended

The addition of white chocolate to the custard makes the pudding **deliciously creamy**. I used Green and Black's white chocolate which contains bourbon vanilla. If you use another chocolate, you could add a teaspoon of vanilla extract or scrape the seeds of a vanilla pod into the custard. No sugar is included as both the brioches and the chocolate are sweet. Serve with some chilled single cream.

WHITE CHOCOLATE BREAD & BUTTER PUDDING

25 g (1 oz) butter, softened
4 brioche, each cut into 4 slices
115 g (4 oz) Green and Black's white chocolate, cut into pieces
300 ml (10 fl oz) double cream
150 ml (5 fl oz) milk
2 eggs
2 egg yolks

1 Lightly butter an ovenproof dish 18 cm x 23 cm (7 inches x 9 inches) and about 5 cm (2 inches) deep. Spread the butter on the brioches slices.

2 Place the chocolate, cream and milk in a bowl and place it over a pan of barely simmering water until the chocolate melts, stirring from time to time. Remove it from the heat. Whisk the eggs and egg yolks together and then whisk this into the chocolate mixture. Spread enough of the custard to cover the base of the dish.

3 Arrange the brioches slices in the dish, overlapping them slightly. Pour the remaining custard over the brioches slices. Press the slices down gently with a spoon to make sure that they are all immersed in the custard. When completely cool, cover with clingfilm and place in the fridge for a minimum of 2 hours.

4 Preheat the oven to Gas Mark 4/electric oven 180°C/fan oven 160°C. Remove the clingfilm and bake in the oven for 30–35 minutes until the brioches is crisp and the white chocolate custard has set.

As you might expect, there is an American influence here with the inclusion of recipes for brownies, muffins and cookies. There are so many variations of these recipes and, as long as you stick to the basic ingredients, you can create your own! It's well worth doubling the ingredients so that you can freeze some – it's great to be able to take some out of the freezer when you have unexpected guests.

SMALL CAKES, BISCUITS & COOKIES

Some of the recipes here are ideal for children to make, with a little help from you. Most of the recipes do not take long to cook, so impatient little ones won't have long to wait to see and taste the result of their endeavours!

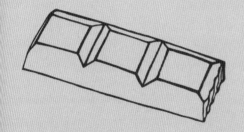 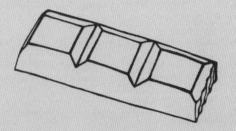 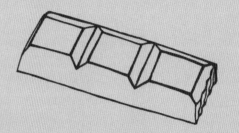

MAKES: 20–24
PREPARATION & COOKING TIME:
20 minutes + 30 minutes cooking
FREEZING: recommended

CHOCOLATE BROWNIES

The addition of white chocolate and walnuts to these brownies make them that little bit extra special. They are best served warm, ideally with some top notch real vanilla ice cream – **a delicious dessert!**

115 g (4 oz) butter, diced
115 g (4 oz) plain chocolate, broken into pieces
1 tablespoon golden syrup
150 g (5 oz) dark muscovado sugar
150 g (5 oz) caster sugar
4 eggs, beaten
225 g (8 oz) self-raising flour
40 g (1½ oz) cocoa powder
50 g (2 oz) white chocolate, cut into small pieces
50 g (2 oz) walnut pieces

1 Line the base and sides of a swiss roll tin (measuring about 30 cm x 22 cm (12 inches x 8½ inches) with baking parchment or greased greaseproof paper.
2 Preheat the oven to Gas Mark 4/electric oven 180°C/fan oven 160°C.
3 Place the butter, chocolate and syrup in a large saucepan and melt together over a gentle heat. Add all the other ingredients and mix thoroughly. Spoon the mixture into the prepared tin and spread evenly into the corners.
4 Bake in the oven for approximately 30 minutes until it has risen, is firm to the touch and coming away from the sides. Allow to cool in the tin.
5 When cold, cut into squares and store in an airtight tin until ready to serve.

MAKES: 24
PREPARATION & COOKING TIME:
30 minutes + 25 minutes cooking
FREEZING: recommended

CHOCOLATE & DATE SQUARES

Including dates in these little cakes make them incredibly moist and seem to accentuate their chocolate flavour. You could mix in some chopped walnuts or pecan nuts to add some crunch.

If you pop them in the fridge in a sealed container for a while before serving, the topping will be **nice and crunchy**.

250 g (9 oz) stoned dates
150 ml (5 fl oz) apple juice
175 g (6 oz) plain chocolate, broken into pieces
115 g (4 oz) soft margarine
115 g (4 oz) dark muscovado sugar
2 eggs, beaten lightly
175 g (6 oz) self-raising flour

FOR THE TOPPING:
175 g (6 oz) white chocolate,
    broken into pieces
80 g (3 oz) unsalted butter
115 g (4 oz) icing sugar, sifted

1 Preheat the oven to Gas Mark 5/electric oven 190°C/fan oven 170°C. Grease a swiss roll tin and line it with greaseproof paper.
2 Place the dates, apple juice and 80 ml (3 fl oz) water in a saucepan, bring to the boil and simmer for 5 minutes. Add the chocolate and stir until melted.
3 Cream the margarine and sugar together until the mixture is fluffy and then beat in the eggs, a little at a time. Fold in the flour and then the date and chocolate mixture until all the ingredients have been incorporated.
4 Spoon the mixture into the prepared tin and spread evenly into the corners. Bake for 20–25 minutes until the cake is risen and firm to the touch, and is coming away from the sides of the tin. Allow to cool in the tin.
5 Meanwhile, make the topping. Place the chocolate and butter in a bowl and place over a pan of barely simmering water and melt, stirring from time to time. Whisk in the icing sugar, a little at a time. Spread over the surface of the cake and leave to set before cutting into squares.

MAKES: 24
PREPARATION TIME: 30 minutes
FREEZING: not recommended

I made these little triangles for my daughter, Holly, to take into school for her 11th birthday. They were a huge success: a couple of parents and her form teacher asked me for the recipe and her friends asked me to make them for her party! They are **ideal for children** to prepare themselves, under supervision.

115 g (4 oz) butter or margarine
115 g (4 oz) marshmallows
115 g (4 oz) toffees
200 g (7 oz) 'Cheerios'
115 g (4 oz) white chocolate, melted
115 g (4 oz) plain chocolate, melted

1   Place the butter or margarine, marshmallows and toffees in a large saucepan and heat very gently, stirring from time to time, until all the ingredients have melted. Remove from the heat, add the 'Cheerios' and stir so that they are coated in the sauce.
2   Spoon into a large (about 30 cm x 23 cm/12 inch x 8½ inch) swiss roll tin. Level the surface spreading the mixture into the corners.
3   Meanwhile melt the chocolates separately – each in a bowl over a pan of barely simmering water.
4   Spoon dollops of the white chocolate at intervals on top of the mixture and then spoon dollops of the plain chocolate in the gaps. Using a palette knife, spread the chocolates to cover the surface, creating a swirled effect. Leave to set
5   Cut into squares and cut the squares in half to create triangles.

HOLLY'S CHOCOLATE CARAMEL TRIANGLES

Homemade cookies are **infinitely superior** to those you can buy in the supermarket. They are easy to make and so well worth the effort, particularly when you smell them baking in the oven! You can vary the cookies by adding nuts and replacing the plain chocolate with white or milk.

MAKES: 20
PREPARATION & COOKING TIME:
20 minutes + 12–15 minutes cooking
FREEZING: recommended

CHOCOLATE CHIP COOKIES

80 g (3 oz) butter, softened
80 g (3 oz) light or dark muscovado sugar
80 g (3 oz) demerara sugar
2.5 ml (½ teaspoon) vanilla extract
1 egg, beaten lightly
175 g (6 oz) self-raising flour
115 g (4 oz) chocolate chips or plain chocolate, cut into small pieces

1 Preheat the oven to Gas Mark 4/electric oven 180°C/fan oven 160°C. Grease two large baking sheets or line them with baking parchment.
2 Cream the butter and sugars together until the mixture is light and creamy. Add the vanilla extract and the egg and mix well.
3 Gradually mix in the flour and then stir in the chocolate chips or pieces. Using a dessertspoon, place spoonfuls on the baking sheets, leaving space for the biscuits to spread while cooking. Press each 'mound' lightly with a fork dipped in flour.

4 Bake in the oven for 12–15 minutes until the cookies are golden in colour.
5 Using a palette knife, carefully lift them on to a wire rack and leave to cool and crisp up.

I think that these little chocolate-coated biscuits are so **delicious** and **elegant** to serve when you have friends around for coffee. They also make a lovely present, particularly at Christmas.

MAKES: 20
PREPARATION & COOKING TIME:
30 minutes + 10 minutes cooking
FREEZING: not recommended

FLORENTINES

50 g (2 oz) butter
50 g (2 oz) demerara sugar
50 g (2 oz) golden syrup
50 g (2 oz) plain flour
25 g (1 oz) flaked almonds
25 g (1 oz) walnut pieces
25 g (1 oz) glacé cherries, chopped finely
25g (1 oz) stem ginger, chopped finely
80 g (3 oz) white chocolate
80 g (3 oz) plain chocolate

1 Preheat the oven to Gas Mark 4/electric oven 180°C/fan oven 160°C. Cut non-stick baking parchment paper to fit two large baking sheets.

2 Place the butter, sugar and syrup in a saucepan and heat gently, stirring occasionally, until the butter has melted. Remove from the heat and add the remaining ingredients, except the two chocolates. Mix thoroughly. Spoon small spoonfuls of the mixture on to the baking sheets, leaving plenty of space for them to spread. Try and ensure that you have at least one piece of cherry in each biscuit.

3 Bake in the oven for 8–10 minutes or until they are golden brown. Allow them to cool and then lift them off the baking parchment, with care, on to the cooling rack with the same side facing upwards.

4 Meanwhile melt the chocolates separately – each in a bowl over a pan of barely simmering water. When the biscuits have cooled completely, turn them over on the cooling rack and spread half of them with white chocolate and the other half with the plain chocolate. Using a fork, make a zig-zag pattern on the chocolate. Leave to set and then store them in an airtight container.

MAKES 8–10
PREPARATION & COOKING TIME:
15 minutes + 20 minutes cooking
FREEZING: recommended

Warm chocolate muffins are **irresistible** – these will be eaten before they have cooled! Don't be tempted to over beat the mixture as they will end up heavy. The taste of the   isn't obvious – it simply adds a depth of flavour to the muffins.

TRIPLE CHOCOLATE MUFFINS

175 g (6 oz) self-raising flour
25 g (1 oz) cocoa powder
2 teaspoons baking powder
50 g (2 oz) dark muscovado sugar
50 g (2 oz) butter, melted
2 eggs, beaten
150 ml (5 fl oz) plain Greek yogurt
30 ml (2 tablespoons) black coffee
15–30 ml (1–2 tablespoons) milk
50 g (2 oz) plain chocolate chips
50 g (2 oz) white chocolate chips
25 g (1 oz) white chocolate, melted (optional)

1 Preheat the oven to Gas Mark 6/electric oven 200°C/fan oven 180°C. Place 10 muffin cases in a muffin tin (you could use ordinary patty tins if you don't have muffin tins).

2 Sift the flour, cocoa powder and baking powder together in a large mixing bowl. Stir in the sugar and then add the melted butter, eggs, yogurt, coffee, 15 ml (1 tablespoon) milk and both chocolate chips. Mix together quickly, adding the rest of the milk if the mixture seems dry.

3 Spoon the mixture into the muffin cases and bake in the oven for 20 minutes, until the muffins have risen and are firm to the touch.

4 Cool on a wire rack. Drizzle the melted white chocolate, if using, across the tops either by pouring it into a small plastic bag and snipping the corner or by using a teaspoon.

In this chapter you will find some unusual and surprising recipes. Here chocolate is used in rather unexpected ways sometimes even in savoury dishes: you can't taste the chocolate in them, but it certainly gives the dish an extra dimension. Try the Vegetarian

UNUSUAL CHOCOLATE RECIPES

Chilli or Chicken Mole and discover the depth and richness dark chocolate adds to the sauce. There's also a pasta recipe, Chocolate Macaroni Pudding, as many children are huge fans of pasta, and with the addition of chocolate you're onto a winner!

SERVES 6
PREPARATION & COOKING TIME: 20 minutes + 2 hours cooking
FREEZING: recommended

APRICOT & CHOCOLATE RICE PUDDING

This rice pudding takes very little time to prepare but benefits from slow cooking, hence the two hours in the oven. The addition of chocolate and dried apricots make an everyday pudding very special. You could even spread some apricot conserve in the base of the dish. Serve this with some some apricot compote or single cream.

300 ml (10 fl oz) single cream
600 ml (1 pint) milk
50 g (2 oz) pudding rice
50 g (2 oz) caster sugar
115 g (4 oz) plain chocolate, broken into pieces
50 g (2 oz) dried apricots, cut into small pieces
25 g (1 oz) butter, cut into small pieces

1 Preheat the oven to Gas Mark 2/electric oven 150°C/fan oven 130°C. Butter an ovenproof dish.
2 Place the cream, milk, rice, sugar and chocolate in a saucepan and heat gently, stirring from time to time, until the chocolate has melted.
3 Scatter the apricots in the prepared dish and pour over the rice mixture. Scatter the butter over the surface.
4 Bake in the oven for 2 hours until the rice is cooked and the liquid has been absorbed.

SERVES 4–6
PREPARATION & COOKING TIME: 20 minutes
FREEZING: recommended

CHOCOLATE MACARONI PUDDING

Most children love pasta in any shape or form. With this in mind, I created a pudding combining macaroni with a chocolate custard sauce. Serve with plenty of cream.

225 g (8 oz) macaroni
2 tablespoons custard powder
2 tablespoons cocoa powder
425 ml (¾ pint) milk
80 g (3 oz) caster sugar
150 ml (5 fl oz) double cream
25 g (1 oz) demerara sugar

1 Cook the macaroni according to the pack instructions. Drain and rinse well.
2 Preheat the oven to Gas Mark 4/electric oven 180°C/fan oven 160°C.
3 Blend the custard and cocoa powders with a little of the milk to form a paste. Add the caster sugar and mix well. Heat the remaining milk and the cream in a saucepan until on the point of boiling and then pour this on to the chocolate custard mixture, while whisking. Return the mixture to the saucepan and heat gently until it thickens. Remove the pan from the heat and fold in the macaroni.
4 Transfer the mixture to a greased gratin dish, sprinkle the surface with the demerara sugar and bake in the oven for 20 minutes or until it is heated through and the topping is crisp and golden.

SERVES 4
PREPARATION & COOKING TIME:
25 minutes + 40 minutes cooking
FREEZING: recommended

ROASTED VEGETABLE CHILLI

I adore roasted vegetables and preparing a vegetarian chilli in this way really brings out the flavour of the vegetables. You can vary the vegetables to suit your tastes and availability. Rice is the usual accompaniment to this dish, but I like it with jacket potatoes served with butter or soured cream. Using a ready-made tomato sauce makes it a fairly speedy meal to prepare.

I aubergine, cut into 2.5 cm (1-inch) pieces
I red and I green pepper, both de-seeded and cut into
   2.5 cm (1-inch) pieces
175 g (6 oz) chestnut mushrooms, wiped and halved
I leek, trimmed and sliced
I red chilli, halved, de-seeded and diced finely
3 garlic cloves, peeled and crushed
60 ml (4 tablespoons) olive oil
420 g can of kidney beans, drained and rinsed
300 g jar of ready-made tomato sauce
50 g (2 oz) plain chocolate, grated
salt and freshly ground black pepper

1. Preheat the oven to Gas Mark 6/electric oven 200°C/fan oven 180°C.
2. Spread the prepared vegetables out in a single layer on two large baking sheets. Scatter the chilli and garlic over them and season with salt and pepper. Drizzle the olive oil over and toss them so that they are all coated in the oil. Bake in the oven for 30–40 minutes until the vegetables are cooked and tinged brown.
3. Place the kidney beans and tomato sauce in a large saucepan and heat through. Add the vegetables to the pan and stir to coat them in the sauce.
4. Add the grated chocolate and simmer gently for a few minutes. Adjust the seasoning, if necessary, and serve.

PREPARATION & COOKING TIME:
20 minutes + 1¾ hours proving
+ 40 minutes cooking
FREEZING: recommended

This bread is very popular in Italy and is usually served with a cream cheese such as mascarpone. **It's a delicious alternative to croissant or pain au chocolat at breakfast.** I like to eat it with a conserve such as apricot.

350 g (12 oz) strong white flour
2 tablespoons cocoa powder
½ teaspoon salt
40 g (1½ oz) icing sugar
15 g (½ oz) fresh yeast
225 ml (8 fl oz) warm water
25 g (1 oz) softened butter
40 g (1½ oz) white chocolate,
broken into small pieces
40 g (1½ oz) plain chocolate,
broken into small pieces
melted butter, for glazing

1 Sift the flour, cocoa and salt into a mixing bowl and stir in the icing sugar. Make a well in the middle.

2 Place the yeast in a bowl, add a little of the water and blend to make a cream. Add the remaining water to the yeast mixture and add this to the flour mixture. Mix together to form a dough. Add the butter and then knead the dough on a floured surface until it is smooth and elastic. Place the dough in a bowl which has been lightly oiled and cover with oiled clingfilm. Place in a warm place, such as an airing cupboard, for about 1 hour until it has doubled in size.

3 Remove the dough from the bowl and place it on the floured surface. Knock the dough back to its original size and knead in the two chocolates. Grease a 15 cm (6-inch) round loose-bottomed cake tin. Shape the dough to fit the tin and place it in the tin. Cover it again with lightly oiled clingfilm and place in the airing cupboard for a further 45 minutes until it has doubled in size again.

4 Preheat the oven to Gas Mark 7/electric oven 220°C/fan oven 200°C and bake for 10 minutes. Reduce the temperature to Gas Mark 5/electric oven 190°C/fan oven 170°C. Bake for a further 25–30 minutes but check it while it is cooking: if the bread is browning too much, cover it loosely with some foil.

5 Remove the bread from the tin, place it on a wire rack to cool and brush the top with melted butter. Leave the bread to cool completely before slicing.

NOTE: If you prefer to use easy-blend dried yeast, add 1 teaspoon to the flour mixture before adding the water.

ITALIAN CHOCOLATE BREAD

SERVES 4
PREPARATION & COOKING TIME:
40 minutes + I hour cooking
FREEZING: recommended

The addition of chocolate to savoury dishes seems odd to us, but it is often added to savoury Mexican dishes and is always added to '**Mole**', Mexico's most famous dish. You could substitute turkey for the chicken. If you do not like too much heat in your food, I suggest that you remove the seeds from the fresh chilli. Serve the dish with some rice and green beans.

CHICKEN MOLE

4 large chicken breasts, skin on
2 garlic cloves, peeled and crushed
I onion, peeled and chopped roughly
½ teaspoon crushed dried chillies
450 ml (16 fl oz) light chicken stock
I fresh red chilli, chopped
80 g (3 oz) flaked almonds
80 g (3 oz) fresh breadcrumbs
I tablespoon sesame seeds
½ teaspoon ground cinnamon
15 ml (I tablespoon) olive oil
400 g can of chopped tomatoes
40 g (1½ oz) plain chocolate,
broken into small pieces
salt and freshly ground black pepper
4 teaspoons sesame seeds, toasted, to serve

I   Place the chicken, garlic, onion and crushed chillies in a large saucepan and add the stock. Bring to the boil, cover and simmer for 40 minutes until the chicken is cooked. Remove the chicken with a slotted spoon and strain the stock, reserving 425 ml (¾ pint). Remove the skin from the chicken and then cut it into large chunks. Cover the chicken and keep warm.

2   Place the fresh chilli, flaked almonds, breadcrumbs, sesame seeds and cinnamon in a blender and process until smooth with about half the reserved stock. Heat the oil in the saucepan and add the blended mixture, frying gently for a couple of minutes. Add the tomatoes and simmer for I minute and then gradually add the remaining stock and chocolate. Simmer gently for 5 minutes, stirring often. Season to taste.

3   Add the chicken to the mixture, bring to the boil and simmer gently for a further 2 minutes. Serve with toasted sesame seeds sprinkled over each portion.